Everyday Assertiveness

*Unlock the Assertive and Confident you,
Stop Pleasing People, Set Healthy
Boundaries and Say NO!*

*(Workbook to Transform your Life &
Communication)*

MASTER.TODAY

Roger Reed

THINGS
I WANTED
TO SAY
BUT
NEVER
DID

Introduction

Assertiveness, the ability to clearly say how you feel and what you want, is an important but often undervalued ability. Learning to become assertive is vital if you are to live a fulfilling and satisfying life. However, although assertiveness is a quality, we have all heard of, there is a great deal of confusion about what it actually means. Many people confuse assertiveness with:

- Aggression
- Selfishness
- Bullying
- Arrogance

Assertiveness does not involve any of these negative attributes. Assertiveness is a series of skills and abilities that allow you to clearly state what is important to you without violating the rights and needs of other people. Above all, assertiveness is a communication skill. To become assertive means learning to express yourself clearly and without causing offense. It means understanding and valuing your own needs as well as those of other people.

Consideration for others is the essential difference between arrogance and assertiveness, for example. Arrogance means exclusively pursuing your own goals. Assertiveness means taking a wider view. Assertiveness is an essential life skill. Every successful person is assertive. We can be certain about this because, if you are not assertive, you will not succeed, no matter now brilliant you are.

Assertiveness is important in every part of our lives. In our careers, we cannot advance or improve without being assertive. In our personal lives, assertiveness leads to more fulfilling and satisfying relationships. In everything we do, the ability to value and clearly communicate our needs is a prerequisite for success.

Being passive is the opposite of being assertive. Being excessively passive not only limits your ability to attain your goals, but it is also unhealthy. Passivity has been shown to lead to low self-esteem, anxiety, and even depression. People who are passive are rarely content. Trying to keep everyone happy will never be possible because people have different wants and needs. You cannot please them all and trying to do so will cause stress.

The good news is that assertiveness is something you can learn. Surprisingly, <u>not</u> being assertive is a behavior that you have learned. You were born assertive. Babies express emotion freely, and they are good at making us understand what they want. You were like that once, but since then, you have learned to hide your own feelings. You have learned to avoid conflict by giving in and ignoring your needs to benefit others. You have learned to become passive.

This book is about relearning the skills you need to become assertive. It explains what assertiveness is, and it provides practical strategies for applying those skills

Becoming assertive is not something that will happen overnight, but you can learn these skills over time.

Are you ready to discover the benefits of becoming assertive?

YOUR FREE GIFT

We would like to give you a gift to thank you for purchasing this book. You can choose from any of our other published titles.

You can get immediate access to any of our books by clicking on the link below and joining our mailing list:

https://campsite.bio/mastertoday

Our other books

Mental Toughness & Discipline Mastery: *Build your Self-Confidence to Unlock your Courage and Resilience*

Find out more here:

https://master.today/books/mental-toughness/

Table of Contents

Part 1: What is Assertiveness and Why Do You Need it?

The first part of this book is about learning where you are right now in regard to assertiveness. We slip into habits of behavior over time without really noticing. Sometimes, we need to stop and take the time to understand where we are now. That practice is not always comfortable. It can be a shock to discover that we aren't the person we thought we were and to realize that somehow, we have drifted far from our core beliefs.

But you must do that if you want to change. You cannot build something new without firm foundations. The fact that you are reading this book means that you want to change. You may be tempted to rush on to the parts of this book that tell you how to become assertive. Instead, take the time to read this part and to think honestly about how it applies to you. Are you striving too hard to be nice? Are you a people-pleaser? Do you have misconceptions about what being assertive means? Are there people in your life who are taking advantage of you and preventing you from achieving your full potential?

Only when you have completed this mental audit will you be ready to apply the techniques that will help you change.

Chapter 1: Are You a Nice Person?

Take a nice test

You better watch out,

You better not cry,

Better not pout,

I'm telling you why...

Santa Claus is Coming to Town

We all want to be nice. First as children, and then as adults, we are told that being nice to other people is an essential social skill. If we aren't nice, people won't like us.

There is nothing wrong with being nice, especially when being polite and considerate toward other people. However, it is possible to be too nice. This tendency can lead to being so concerned about making sure others are happy that we forget about our own needs. We can find ourselves feeling resentful, angry, and even depressed because no matter how hard we try, we can never seem to be able to please everyone.

Given that you are reading this book, perhaps that's how you feel? Do you feel that you spend all your time trying to please others? Yet, no matter how much you do, they always seem to want more. Do you spend so much time thinking about what other people want that you never seem to have time to consider your own needs?

Perhaps you are trying too hard to be nice.

Take this simple test. This isn't intended as a scientific or psychological test. It is just a method for making you think about your behavior in terms of assertiveness now. Be honest!

1. You order food in a restaurant. When your food arrives, it isn't what you ordered. Do you:
   a. Say nothing. It will probably be fine, and you don't want to spoil the evening for everyone else.
   b. Mention it to the people you are dining with but eat it anyway.
   c. Tell the server they have made a mistake and ask them to give you the correct order.
2. Someone pushes ahead of you in a line. Do you:
   a. Say nothing. They're probably in more of a hurry than you are.
   b. Sigh in an exasperated way but don't say anything.
   c. Tell the person, *"Excuse me, but I believe I was ahead of you."*
3. You are in a supermarket. Someone barges their shopping cart into you from behind. Do you:
   a. Apologize.
   b. Say nothing but look hard at them.
   c. Tell the person, *"Please be careful."*
4. You are with a group of friends and someone says something that you disagree with. Perhaps it's even something you find offensive. Do you:
   a. Say nothing. You don't want to offend them or start an argument.
   b. Gently say that you disagree.

    c.   Tell them firmly that you disagree and explain why you think they are mistaken.

5. How often do you feel guilty?
    a. All the time.
    b. Only occasionally.
    c. Never.
6. If someone asks you for a favor, how often do you refuse?
    a. Never.
    b. Occasionally.
    c. All the time.
7. You and a friend or partner are planning an evening out. You disagree on where to go. How does that usually work out?
    a. I usually go along with what they want.
    b. Sometimes I do what they want, sometimes they do what I want.
    c. We always do what I want.

If your answers are generally "*a,*" you may be too nice. You are unwilling or unable to assert yourself even when that would be a perfectly reasonable response. If your answers are generally "*b,*" you may still be a little too nice. If your answers are all "*c,*" you certainly aren't too nice, and you are already assertive.

Can you really be too nice, and if so, is that a problem? The answers you gave in the test above are only a guide. The most significant question to ask yourself is how does being consistently nice make you feel? If you feel confident, relaxed, and fulfilled, then clearly your current level of assertiveness isn't a problem. But for many people, being too nice is a problem because it leaves them feeling used, taken advantage of, resentful, and unfulfilled.

It's also true that nice people often attract friends who take advantage of them. A person who always wants to get their own way will be attracted to a passive person. A lazy person will seek out those who will serve them. People who are consistently nice believe that always doing what others want will make people like them. That is not true.

Let's take a look at why the desire to be liked is such a powerful driver of human behavior.

Human interaction is essential to our mental and physical wellbeing. Humans are social creatures and without interaction, we suffer. In its most ancient forms, cooperation in human society was the only way to survive. That is why the need for interaction is hardwired into the human brain.

A well-known story about Frederick II, Emperor of the Holy Roman Empire in the 13th century, illustrates this need for human interaction. Frederick wanted to undertake an experiment to answer one of the most important theological questions of the time: what language did Adam and Eve speak? To find an answer, Frederick had several infants raised by foster mothers who looked after the children's physical needs but were forbidden from conversing with the infants or even speaking within their hearing. Frederick believed that somehow, the original language inspired by God would spontaneously arise in these children. Instead, all the children weakened and died.

That may be an apocryphal story, but its premise is confirmed by many more recent scientific studies. These studies show that social interactions, how we react to people around us, improve cognitive ability as well as mental and physical health. A significant part of these interactions is our desire for approval, appreciation, and acceptance by others. This also appears to have direct implications for our physical wellbeing. A nine-year study of thousands of people undertaken in Alameda County,

California[1] found that people with close social ties lived notably longer, even when they had unhealthy lifestyle choices that included smoking, obesity, and a lack of exercise. Studies such as this confirm that we all need to feel that we are part of something and accepted as part of a social group. That is why we all have a fundamental need to be liked.

This can become a problem if we give in to a need to be liked by everyone. In practical terms, that is never going to be possible. No person will be liked by everyone, and people who struggle to make everyone like them are often suffering from problems with low self-esteem. These may originate from issues during childhood or as a result of emotional or physical abuse in adult relationships.

Like many other issues that affect mental health, the need to be liked only becomes a problem when it is compulsive. Most people would prefer to be liked rather than disliked. You have a problem when you have a compulsive need to be liked by everyone. If you suffer from this compulsive need, then you are inevitably headed for disappointment and resentment.

You may even find that you are becoming a people-pleaser.

---

[11] Lisa F. Berkman, S. Leonard Syme, *SOCIAL NETWORKS, HOST RESISTANCE, AND MORTALITY: A NINE-YEAR FOLLOW-UP STUDY OF ALAMEDA COUNTY RESIDENTS*, American Journal of Epidemiology, February 1979.

Social psychologist and author Susan Newman, Ph.D. used the term *"people-pleaser[2]"* to describe anyone who has a compulsive need to make other people happy. People-pleasers constantly seek outside validation. They lack self-confidence and see their own self-worth only as it is reflected in the approval of others.

Of course, a desire to please other people and to be liked by them is not in itself harmful. Any effective relationship involves understanding and considering other people's needs and feelings. This only becomes a problem when our desire to make other people happy makes us ignore or disregard our own needs and feelings.

How can you tell if you are a people-pleaser?

> **Do you ever pretend to agree with people?** Listening to other people is an important social skill. Being polite and attentive when another person is speaking is a good way to let them know that you are really listening. But people-pleasers often find themselves pretending to agree with the other person simply to make them happy.
>
> **Do you feel uncomfortable if someone is unhappy?** Anyone with empathy and compassion will relate if a friend or colleague is unhappy. People-pleasers feel that the other person's unhappiness is somehow their fault and that they

---

2 *The Book of No: 250 Ways to Say It—And Mean It and Stop People-Pleasing Forever*, Susan Newman, McGraw-Hill, 2005.

are responsible. If you feel guilty about another person's unhappiness even though you have not caused that feeling, you may be a people-pleaser.

Do you find it difficult to give honest opinions? We have all been in the situation where a friend, partner, or colleague asks us for advice. Sometimes, we know that the advice we should give may be unwelcome or even painful. What do you do in those circumstances? If you genuinely believe that the person asking for advice will benefit from hearing what you have to say, you will say it. If you are a people-pleaser, you will say whatever is needed to make the person you are talking to happy, not give them the best advice.

Do you adopt unhelpful behaviors just to make other people happy? A number of studies show that people-pleasers engage in unhealthy and even destructive behaviors because they feel that this will make others feel more comfortable in social situations. This tendency can cover a range of behaviors from excessive drinking or eating to aggression. Adopting these behaviors often makes people-pleasers feel bad, but they feel compelled to act in this way because other people in their social group are acting in these ways

Will you do anything to avoid conflict? Some level of conflict is a normal part of social interaction. No two people will ever totally agree about everything. Debate and discussion during which you defend your point of view is healthy and productive. People-pleasers do not see it that way. They will do anything to avoid conflict of any sort. They see conflict as a symptom of unhappiness, and they believe it is somehow their fault.

Are your incapable of saying *"No?"* No one likes turning down a request for help or time from a friend. However, people-pleasers seem congenitally incapable of saying *"No"* in any circumstance. They will agree to almost anything, even if that agreement leaves them stressed and resentful.

Like many other concepts in this book, being a people-pleaser is not an all-or-nothing condition. You may find that you are more likely to adopt some of the behaviors noted above with a particular group or even a particular person. Perhaps you only find yourself behaving in this way with your partner or boss. This activity is not intended as a checklist with a score to decide if you are a people-pleaser. It is   intended to make you think about your own behavior to see if you can identify with any people-pleasing traits

Being a people-pleaser is not itself a problem. However, it is a strong indicator that you may have underlying issues of self-esteem and a lack of assertiveness. Being nice has a price.

Being nice has a price

What is wrong with being a people-pleaser, with being consistently nice to everyone, all the time? There are two different answers to this, one practical and one psychological. Let's start with looking at practical reasons why people-pleasers aren't generally respected or even liked.

If you always agree and never say anything unpleasant, you might think that would make people like you. It doesn't. People will instead quickly begin to doubt your sincerity and honesty. Part of the reason for this is that, while your words may say "*I agree*," your body language and other non-verbal cues you subconsciously provide are clearly saying "*I disagree*." People are particularly good at picking up these non-verbal messages, even though they may not be aware of doing this. When they are confronted with a person who is saying one thing but giving messages that suggest the opposite, they are very unlikely to trust this person or respect what they say.

If you constantly give praise and positive affirmation, your words will become devalued. If you give honest responses, people will value those that are positive far more than they will the bland, all-encompassing encouragement they get from a people-pleaser.

People-pleasers are actually avoiding intimacy. By carefully censoring everything you say to remove anything that may make the person you are talking to unhappy, you restrict your social interactions to the most superficial level. Real intimacy involves honesty. People-pleasers are incapable of honesty, and their social interactions can never be truly satisfying. Other people become aware of this lack of sincerity and they will never value the friendship of a people-pleaser as much as that of someone who is honest.

Think about someone you know who is a people-pleaser. Most of us know at least one. How do you feel about them? Do you value spending time with them? Do you look forward to chatting with them? Or do you find their bland chatter rather dull? If you are a people-pleaser, it's very possible that is how others think of you.

However, beyond the negative reactions that being a people-pleaser causes in others, it also has direct and unhelpful psychological implications for you. The dissonance between what you say and what you really think may lead you to feeling like an imposter. You know that what you are saying is not true, but you cannot bring yourself to assert what you really feel.

This habit can lead to your feeling alienated from your true self and your life values. People-pleasers' sense of self-worth comes entirely from the opinions of others. Underneath, they suspect that they may not be likeable. But they fight this fear by acting in ways that are specifically intended to make others like them. This habit makes them feel likeable. Acting in this way is not healthy. To be constantly likeable to everyone, we must crush whole segments of our personality. We cannot show anger, competitiveness, or even disagreement because we fear that these may make people like us less. We must become so bland that we do not risk offending anyone.

Being forced to act in false ways is the real price of nice. You may find yourself restricted to shallow, unsatisfying relationships. These relationships may be with people you do not even like, but you still want their approval. You may find yourself acting and speaking in ways that do not accord with your inner values. You may find yourself feeling resentful and frustrated.

The good news is that you do not have to continue like this. By learning to become more assertive, you can improve your own mental health and have meaningful relationships. But before we begin talking about how to become more assertive, we need to stop for a moment. Let's think about the basic rights we have that we may have lost sight of in our constant pursuit of being nice.

Almost all of us strive to be nice, consciously, or subconsciously. We do this even though we are often unclear about what "nice" means. We are simply conditioned by society to act in ways that support the needs of other people while ignoring our own. This chapter has been about understanding why that desire may be counterproductive or even unhealthy.

There is something else important that you need to consider here: You have the right to look after yourself.

It has even been said that each of us has not just a right, but also a responsibility to look after ourselves. Kristi Ling, writer, happiness expert, and author of the bestselling book *Operation Happiness* notes:

"Caring for your body, mind, and spirit is your greatest and grandest responsibility."

Think of those safety placards you see when you travel on an airplane. The ones that tell you to put on your own oxygen mask before trying to help anyone else. That might sound selfish, but it's really the best way to act. If you ignore that instruction and try to help someone else with their mask first, you may become incapacitated. Then you won't be able to help them at all, and you will both suffer.

Perhaps everyday life should come with one of those safety placards, too? If you spend all your time trying to please other people and you ignore your own needs, you will almost certainly end up beaten down, resentful, guilty, and perhaps even depressed. Doesn't it make more sense to look after your own needs first, which will make you stronger, more resilient, and better able to effectively look after others? Looking after your own needs (and that is really what assertiveness is about) helps you and everyone around you.

We'll come back to each of these in more detail later, but for the moment, consider these basic rights that all of us are entitled to:

> **You have the right to be happy.** The wise men who created the declaration upon which the United States was founded noted three inherent and inalienable rights: *"The preservation of life, and liberty, and the pursuit of happiness."* Those rights apply to you. You have the right to pursue happiness. That isn't selfish, wicked, or self-indulgent. In part, it's what defines us as human beings. To understand what makes you happy and to assert your right to it is partly what this book is about.

> **You have the right to say "no."** We all have busy lives where we juggle conflicting demands on our time and energy. These demands can leave us feeling exhausted and dissatisfied. You must recognize that you have the right to look after yourself and that you cannot do everything for everyone. That means you are going to have to learn to say *"No"* to some of those demands on your time. That's tough. Many of us find it exceedingly difficult to say "no." Understanding that doing so is necessary and learning how to do

it is an essential step towards learning to be assertive.

You don't have to judge your life by other people's standards. Everyone has different needs and goals. These mean that people have vastly different judgements about what represents success and achievement in life. If you spend too much time listening to what other people expect of you may lose touch with what really matters to you. Don't let that happen. Stay focused on the goals that matter to you and learn to ignore people who judge you by different standards.

You don't have to justify your behavior. Something you will learn in this book is to recognize what is important to you. Of course, there will always be other elements competing for your time and attention. But if playing golf or spending time with your cat are what make you feel good, you don't have to find excuses for fitting those activities into your schedule.

You are a nice person. You like to make everyone happy. You help anyone who asks. If this describes you, the four statements above probably make you feel uncomfortable, especially the first one. Your own happiness may not be something you usually focus on. But that must change. You must look after yourself, understand your own needs, and learn how to assert yourself in order to fulfil those needs.

Of course, there is an important corollary here. Other people have these same rights, too. Fortunately, being assertive does not mean ignoring other people's needs and feelings. On the contrary, it means taking these into account, but not allowing them to always take priority over your own rights. You can still be nice while you're being assertive. In fact, learning to assert yourself may help to make you even nicer than you are now!

You can do
the hard
things.

Chapter 2: What is Assertiveness?

What do we mean by "assertive"?

Before we go any further, it is worth pausing for a moment to explain precisely what is meant by *"assertiveness."*

Learning to be assertive does not mean that you will automatically get everything you want. Other people have the right to be assertive, too, and they may not have the same needs or goals. Learning to be assertive is not a secret technique that will make you wealthy and successful. You will still have to be prepared to cooperate and negotiate with other people in order to find a way forward that satisfies everyone.

Learning to be assertive means understanding and recognizing your own needs and feelings and being able to communicate these without aggression. It means learning to stand up for your own rights while respecting the rights of others. It involves deeper and more satisfying relationships and coming to see the world in a more positive way.

If you can learn to become assertive, you won't always get your own way, but you will increase your self-image and self-esteem, and you will be able to treat other people in a respectful way.

In theory, we all value the quality of "niceness." We appreciate nice people, and we ourselves generally strive to behave in the same way to others. Being nice is generally seen as something admirable, and perhaps you are worried that you must give up being nice in order to become assertive.

One of the problems is that "nice" is one of those terms that has different meanings to different people. Christianity is one of the most important forces that has shaped thinking in the western world. It has also helped to define what most people think of as the meaning of being nice. Let's look at some of the reasons why nice and assertive are vastly different but also why assertiveness isn't necessarily the opposite of nice.

> **Nice people don't succeed**. In general, modern Christianity is based on tenets that include forgiveness, compassion, and charity. Those are fine qualities. They're what most people regard as nice. However, Christian teaching also came to equate the quality of being nice as being the opposite of being successful. To be successful, you could not be nice and conversely, nice people did not succeed. A successful pursuit of worldly ambitions, for example, became seen as the antithesis of nice. Assertiveness is in part about learning how to get what you want, and for that reason, it can also be seen as the opposite of nice. This is not true. Assertiveness is completely compatible with qualities such as respect for others, compassion, and empathy. Assertive

people are more likely to succeed, but that doesn't mean that they have to be nasty. You can be both succeed and be nice.

Nice people are meek. The Bible tells us *"Blessed are the meek, for they will inherit the earth"* (Matthew 5:5). Meek is often cited as an admirable quality in the Bible but, what is meek? At least one current dictionary defines meek as *"deficient in spirit and courage, submissive.*[3]*"* Does that mean you have to be fearful and submissive to be nice? No! The original Biblical use of this word was based on a quite different meaning. It included compassion but also a steadfast adherence to a course of action, even in the face of adversity. That original meaning of meek is absolutely completely compatible with assertiveness. The modern meaning of meek, which implies passivity, is not.

Nice people are boring. This idea comes from a quite different route, the Romantic movement that began around 1800. Poets such as Byron and Shelly and writers including Sir Walter Scott produced a range of popular works that introduced the "Romantic hero." These emphasized that interesting and exciting people are spontaneous, emotional, troubled, unpredictable, and changeable. This movement

---

[3] Definition from *Merriam-Webster Online Dictionary* (http://www.merriam-webster.com/dictionary/meekness). Retrieved April 15th, 2021.

had a huge influence on every aspect of the creative the arts that persists to the present day. As confirmation, try to name a single movie or television protagonist who is not a classic Romantic hero, troubled and rebellious. There are very few! The opposite of the Romantic hero is the person who is steadfast, dependable, quiet, and consistent. Romanticism tells us that people like this are also boring. Clearly, that is not so. Think of someone you know who you would describe as "assertive." Is that person boring? No!

Can you be both nice and assertive? If you use the term nice to embody positive connotations like compassion, honesty, persistence, and empathy, it is most certainly compatible with assertiveness.

Part of the problem here is that the word assertiveness has itself gained some negative connotations. Many people take it as a synonym for aggression, bullying, or simply as a way of describing selfishness. This is not true. Assertiveness is about learning how to stay true to your inner beliefs as well as understanding how to communicate honestly without alienating and upsetting other people.

Assertive is not the same as aggressive

One of the most common misapprehensions about assertiveness is that it is the same as aggression. It is easy to see why. Both attitudes involve clearly stating your own needs and trying to attain your goals. However, there is a fundamental and essential difference:

- **Aggression means pursuing your own goals without consideration for others.** Aggressive people either ignore the other person's point of view completely, or they are dismissive, disrespectful, or even abusive towards others. Aggression can alienate other people and increase stress in any situation. Studies show[4] that people who behave aggressively have a higher incidence of failed relationships and less support in social and professional groups. Interestingly, the same studies show that aggressive people feel additional stress. They often do not understand the effect their aggression has on other people and they are surprised by negative reactions. They may react by feeling victimized, and this can make them act even more aggressively.
- **Assertiveness means clearly stating your own views while respecting those of others.** Assertiveness means seeking compromise where

---

[4] *Who's Stressed? Distributions of Psychological Stress in the United States in Probability Samples from 1983, 2006, and 2009*, Sheldon Cohen, *Journal of Applied Social Psychology*, Volume 42, Issue 6, June 2012.

necessary and listening to other people. It means looking for solutions that mean everyone wins, not only situations where you prevail. Perhaps surprisingly, studies show that people who have learned to be assertive tend to suffer from less stress, have fewer conflicts in their lives, and suffer from fewer failed relationships[5].

Assertiveness is a helpful and positive attribute while aggression is not. Assertiveness is rooted in respect for others while aggression is negative, divisive, and combative.

Consider a situation where you were involved in a discussion where there has been a difference of opinion or perhaps even a confrontation. This could be a work situation or a personal conflict. What did you say? The following are examples of aggressive statements you might have said:

- You're wrong.
- You don't know what you are talking about.
- You're stupid.
- If we had done it the way I suggested, it would have worked.
- It's your fault.
- You don't understand.

What all these statements have in common is that they are attacking another person and seeking to ascribe blame. They are personal and imply that you are right,

---

[5] *Finding your voice: Reclaiming personal power through communication*, Jane Downing, Allen & Unwin, 1995.

and the other person is wrong. All of them are self-centered and do not take account of the views or feelings of the other person. An aggressive person is loud and challenging and will often use intense eye contact. They're also usually poor listeners who frequently interrupt, criticize, and humiliate others. Naturally, this behavior generates extremely negative responses in people who are forced to interact with them. This behavior tends to make any conflict escalate.

In contrast, the following statements are assertive:

- What have we learned from this?
- What positive outcomes can we take from this?
- Next time, we could...
- What do you think we should do?
- It was my fault.

All these statements stress the collective. They talk about "we" rather than "I." They take account of other people's views while still seeking solutions. They don't seek to ascribe blame but to find something positive to take away from the situation. The last statement is particularly interesting. On the surface, admitting you are to blame does not sound assertive at all. In fact, it seems passive. However, the ability to recognize and admit that you have made a mistake takes great self-confidence. This attitude is also an important part of self-improvement. If you feel that you have nothing to learn, you cannot improve. Mistakes and failures provide some of the best learning opportunities. Assertive people can admit to making mistakes without losing respect. Aggressive people will never admit to making mistakes and will always seek to place blame on other people. Aggressive people do not learn from mistakes.

Hopefully, you can now clearly see the difference between aggression and assertiveness. While you strive to build your assertiveness, you must avoid slipping into aggression. To tell the difference, ask yourself whether your actions make the situation better and lead towards solutions. If they do, you are probably being assertive. If your actions are about blaming others, making yourself look good, and making other people unhappy, you are probably being aggressive.

You should also avoid aggression because it is counterproductive. Aggressive people who use bullying tactics may seem to get what they want, but that strategy is rarely sustainable in the long-term. Aggression prompts negative responses. No one wants to spend time with an aggressive person, and such people often end up excluded and ignored. Assertive people are also able to achieve their goals, but they do so without alienating others around them.

Assertiveness is positive and solution-focused, and it prompts respect. Aggression is negative. It is often rooted in insecurity and anxiety and it leads to dislike and avoidance. Know the difference and continually assess your behavior to guard against aggression.

BigBelly
SOLAR
DON'T
BE
AFRAID
OF
ANYONE

There are a number of recognized benefits that come from learning to be assertive. Let's look at four of the most important.

> **Improved Self-Image.** Self-image is an important concept in mental wellbeing. It comprises your physical view of yourself, what you see when you look in the mirror. But it also involves how you imagine yourself inside your own head. Here is one definition of self-image:
>
> > *"Self-image is how you perceive yourself. It is a number of self-impressions that have built up over time. These self-images can be incredibly positive, giving a person confidence in their thoughts and actions, or negative, making a person doubtful of their capabilities and ideas.[6]"*
>
> Self-image often involves comparing ourselves with other people. We assess our own perceived attractiveness and success by looking at others. This comparison can be unbalanced by aggression, which leads us to see everyone as inferior to us, or by passivity, seeing everyone else as superior to us. Neither is helpful or heathy.

---

[6] *Mountain State Centers for Independent Living*, website http://mtstcil.org/

Assertiveness allows you to communicate your own needs and preferences, but it also encourages you to consider the same feelings in others. This helps you to see that other people's needs are different to your own. This ability in turn helps you to accept that you cannot please other people all the time and that your own needs are relevant and important. That leads to a more balanced self-image.

Improved self-esteem. Self-image is how we see ourselves. Self-esteem is about how we feel about that image. Self-esteem is concerned with how much respect we have for ourselves and how much we value our own feelings and opinions. Assertiveness teaches us that we have a right to those feelings and shows us how to express them. Assertiveness also leads us to understand that our opinions have value even if someone else disagrees with them.

People-pleasers have such low self-esteem that they are afraid to express opinions. This fear is partly due to worries that saying how they feel will make other people unhappy. Partly it is because they feel that what they feel has no value and is not worth expressing. Learning to be assertive boosts self-esteem.

Improved understanding of other people. People-pleasers have very little real understanding of other people's needs or feelings. Their interactions are superficial and based only on responding in ways that will make the other person happy. Generally, this means agreeing and not gaining a deep understanding of what that person is feeling.

Assertive people do not simply agree all the time. While they may still be supportive, they may also question beliefs and suggest alternate behaviors. Assertive people also understand that other people may have different opinions and can make conscious choices about feelings. Assertive people tend to have a better understanding of their own feelings and this makes them better able to recognize and understand these feelings in other people. Assertive people generally have a much higher chance of developing honest and mutually supportive relationships.

Improved energy. Aggressive people see other people as a threat and waste time and energy on unnecessary conflict. Passive people avoid all conflict but often spend time on guilt. Both these attitudes take mental energy that could be better spent on positive actions.

Assertive people are solution-focused. They know what they want, and they know how to communicate this need. However, they do not see differences of opinion or even conflict as a personal attack, and they seek resolution through action. Being too passive or aggressive wastes mental energy on dealing with imagined problems. Being assertive helps you to see and focus on what really matters and to spend your energy wisely.

Once you understand what assertiveness is, you can see the benefits it brings. However, many people react to this knowledge almost with despair. They can see the benefits, but they just aren't assertive! They feel that they were born passive and that there is nothing they can do about that. Fortunately, this is simply a misunderstanding. Assertiveness comprises a set of skills that anyone can learn.

Assertiveness as a learned skill

Many people reject the notion of learning to become more assertive by claiming that they are just naturally passive or aggressive. In Part 2 of this book, we will give you skills and techniques you can use to increase your assertiveness. The important thing to accept at this stage is that how you are at the moment is not fixed and innate.

Whether you are passive or aggressive, you were not born that way. You learned that behavior. Humans are hardwired with a need for social acceptance. In the early days of the human race that need was essential. Alone, it was not possible to build shelter, find sufficient food, or hunt. Only as part of a group could people survive. We are no longer fighting saber-toothed cats or, generally, concerned with day-to-day survival. However, our need to be accepted by a group is just as strong.

No child is born aggressive or passive. These are behaviors we learn as we grow and seek to ingratiate ourselves with a group. Some children learn to bully those around them while others become submissive in the hope that will make them liked by the group. Neither are good long-term strategies, but they seem to offer instant access to a group.

As we grow, these feelings are reinforced. We still feel the need for acceptance by colleagues, friends, and partners. Many people get stuck in the same way of doing this, either by aggression or submission. However, access to larger and more complex social groups make these techniques less effective. An aggressive bully may be able to make other children do what he wants in the playground, but that same approach will not work well in an adult environment.

So, when you claim that you are just naturally passive, that's not really true. This is something you have learned over time as a strategy to enable you to get along with other people. Your self-image has become distorted. Just as there are mental disorders concerned with how we see our physical selves such as Body Dysmorphic Disorder (BDD), there are distortions in how we perceive our worth and value.

Becoming assertive involves dealing with those distortions of self-image and learning to accept that your needs and feelings have value and importance. Simply using the techniques of assertiveness can actually help to overcome those distortions. By recognizing your feelings and communicating them to others, you can develop new mental pathways, or new ways of thinking that are positive and helpful.

If you feel that you lack assertiveness, accept that this deficiency is not a fixed facet of your personality. You learned to be this way. Happily, you can unlearn it too. It won't be easy, and it will take time, but you can change the way that you think and behave to become more assertive.

We all have beliefs that govern our behavior. These are largely automatic and habitual responses to circumstances, and we are often not even aware that particular beliefs are causing us to act in certain ways. Sometimes, these can be *toxic* self-limiting, self-defeating beliefs that undermine what we are trying to achieve.

In this chapter we will examine some of the most toxic beliefs. When you are reading, think about whether these apply to you. Later, we will provide specific techniques and approaches for dealing with these issues.

The need to please

We teach children the importance of sharing and considering other people's needs. Learning about compassion and generosity are important parts of developing as a person, but sometimes, this teaching can lead to a belief that it is selfish to value your own needs. It can also lead to basing our self-image and self-esteem entirely on how much we please others.

We are social creatures and learning to care about other people is important. But if the need to please becomes dominant, it can skew our thinking and lead to viewing everything we do in terms of how it affects other people, not what it does for us.

In extreme cases, people suffering from this from of distorted thinking feel that they are responsible for the happiness of others. If someone is unhappy, these people feel guilty because they believe themselves to be somehow responsible for that unhappiness. This guilt can be a powerful driver of behavior even when it is not based on any objective reality. When it is combined with additional guilt when you do occasionally put yourself first, this stress can lead to mental health problems.

People who are affected by an extreme need to please also tend to have poor relationships. Normal, healthy relationships involve give and take on both sides. People-pleasers are completely committed to ensuring the happiness of the other person. That approach might sound as if it should work, but it almost never does. The other person in the relationship will usually come to regard submission and the need to please as routine.

They will rarely respect the other person and generally won't be grateful for attempts to please because these are expected. The people-pleaser will often feel resentful because their acts of kindness don't seem to be recognized, and they may feel guilty about this resentment. The relationship itself will never be more than superficial because the people-pleaser can never be honest for fear that this may cause the other person to be unhappy.

Wanting the significant people in your life to be happy is normal and positive. Feeling that you are entirely responsible for this situation and ignoring your own needs is destructive. Taken to extremes, the need to please can be one of the most damaging and limiting of all the toxic beliefs.

Insecurity and self-doubt

Many people suffer from a poor self-image and low self-esteem. These feelings have many roots in childhood experiences to previous adult relationships, but they can undermine almost everything you do.

If you feel that you are unworthy of love, respect, or even being liked, you will be constantly looking for signs of rejection. In order to avoid the possibility of rejection, you will act in ways intended never to make other people unhappy. You believe that the only way to ensure that people like you is to constantly please them.

You never feel able to assert yourself because that openness might upset other people. And, if they are not happy, you feel that they are more likely to reject you. You become completely submissive because that seems to be the only way to continue to receive love and affection.

People suffering from self-doubt and insecurity are incapable of enjoying normal, healthy relationships. They are constantly on-guard for signs of rejection or disapproval and see these everywhere, even in the most innocuous comments and actions. They brood and make themselves even more submissive in an attempt to become indispensable to the other person. These are the people we are referring to when we use terms like *"clingy."*

Insecure people are emotionally needy and constantly in need of reassurance. Those demands become trying and their unwillingness to be honest limits their relationships to the most superficial level. Insecurity and self-doubt can undermine any relationship.

The need to be good

As children, we are taught that to be "good" is a central part of how we are regarded and valued by others. There is no higher praise for a young child than to be told that they have been good. Being good generally means pleasing others by doing what you are told and showing generosity and compassion for other people's feelings.

These are all positive attributes, and they are an important part of allowing children to learn how to move on from the innate selfishness of the very young. However, these beliefs can become distorted when any focus on self becomes equated with "bad."

When this happens, a belief emerges that the only way to be a good person is to please others. This belief builds to a presumption that if you are selfless all the time and you completely ignore your own feelings in order to focus on the needs of others, that is good. If you also feel guilty about accepting and acting on your own needs, then you are in danger of developing a very distorted view of the world and your place in it.

Your needs and feelings are real. You have the right to seek happiness by seeking to fulfill these needs. Ignoring these feelings completely does not make you a good person. Instead, it makes you a person who has completely lost touch with their real core beliefs. Complete selfishness is unhealthy and negative. Some degree of self-regard and self-interest is not just normal, it's a central part of mental wellbeing.

Few people relish conflict, but for some people, the fear of any form of confrontation can become so crippling that it inhibits everything they do. There are many reasons for this, and they range from childhood experiences, to past relationships, to a fear of upsetting people or feelings that your opinion is worthless. Whatever the cause, if fear of confrontation is allowed to grow unchecked, it can become a major problem.

Confrontation does not necessarily mean fighting or even disagreement. For some people, any conversation that involves raised levels of emotion can seem like a confrontation. They see raised emotion as carrying a risk of anger, unhappiness, and rejection.

They cope by doing anything necessary to avoid confrontation. As soon as someone shows the first sign of emotion, they become submissive and do everything they can to restore calm. The problem is that no matter how compliant and submissive any individual makes themselves, some level of confrontation is inevitable Human beings are individuals with their own needs, motivations, and desires. These differences make some level of confrontation certain in both personal and work environments.

You cannot make yourself so submissive that you can avoid confrontation with everyone all of the time. Some level of disagreement and confrontation is a part of normal social interaction. Unless you learn to develop strategies to deal with confrontation, you will suffer from constant anxiety and stress.

Being assertive is nasty!

A significant barrier that stops people from trying to become more assertive is the notion that this quality is somehow unpleasant. They feel that it is somehow uncaring and rude to say what you want and utterly selfish to set out to attain that.

Having read this far, you should understand that this is a fallacy. Assertiveness means learning to value and communicate your own feelings and needs but adopting that approach does not mean that you will ignore how everyone else around you feels. Life is about compromise, and assertiveness gives you the skills and techniques to ensure that you approach everything you do in a balanced and positive way.

It is not wrong to consider your own feelings. Being a balanced and capable person begins with being fully in touch with your own core beliefs. Doing this gives you focus and goals to work towards. Without those goals, you will be lost and adrift in a world of uncertainty and insecurity. With clear goals, you will know who you are and what makes you happy.

Being assertive is not nasty. It is about finding out who you are and learning to express those values in ways that other people will understand and respect. Your desire to help and support other people is not incompatible with assertiveness. Becoming assertive will make you a happier, more rounded person. In the long term, that makes you more, not less, willing, and able to help others.

It's not my fault!

There is one toxic belief that is very prevalent. This is the feeling that other people are responsible for your happiness. That is untrue. A fundamental element of assertiveness and good mental health is accepting that you alone are responsible for your own happiness.

Happiness is an emotion. It is not simply a reaction to external events. Happiness is based on your perception of those events. No other person can change that perception for you or make it better. *"Find someone who makes you happy"* is a common piece of advice, but it is fundamentally wrong. Other people cannot make you happy, though they can make you unhappy!

Happiness exists only within your own mind. Generally, it comes from actions and experiences that align with your inner values. When you find what experiences make you happy, you may be lucky enough to find another person who shares the same values and who is made happy by the same experiences. These shared sentiments are a strong basis for any friendship or relationship.

Your relationship with other people is based upon your relationship with yourself. If you feel resentful, guilty, insecure, or anxious, those feelings will be projected into all your relationships. If you feel content with yourself and understand what truly makes you happy, you will be far more capable of forming satisfying relationships. Happiness isn't just a vague aspiration. It is the foundation of a fulfilling life. Seeking happiness is a choice you make. Take responsibility for that choice.

Chapter 4: Is Other People's Behavior Harming You?

In the last chapter, we looked at how some of your own beliefs can impact your ability to live a satisfying life and have fulfilling relationships. Having positive self-beliefs is important but, your work and personal relationships involve other people, and their beliefs can also have a significant impact on how you feel.

In this chapter, we will look at some common but unhelpful behaviors that you may encounter in other people. You will see that the more you suffer from the toxic beliefs detailed in the previous chapter, the more vulnerable you are to other people's manipulative behavior. Later, we will tell you how to deal with these behaviors, but for the moment, read this chapter and see if you can identify any of these traits in people you know.

Manipulating guilt

Some people seem to be experts at exploiting your guilt and using those emotions to get you to do what they want. Using guilt in this way, "guilt-tripping," is recognized as a form of emotional manipulation. Some psychologists go further, identifying it as a form of bullying or even of abuse. How can you recognize when someone is using guilt to manipulate you?

Let's begin by defining what we mean by guilt. The words "*guilt*" and "*shame*" are often used interchangeably in conversation, but when they are used as psychological terms, they are different. Shame is an internal reaction based on our failing to conform to our self-image. Guilt is regret about how we have treated someone else. Imagine you are at a social gathering and you say something deliberately hurtful to someone. You may feel shame because you like to imagine that you are not the kind of person who does that. You also feel guilty because of the pain that you caused to the other person. Shame is entirely based on our own inner values which may not be readily obvious to someone on the outside. Guilt is easier to manipulate because it arises from external circumstances.

In the example above, it's normal to feel guilty for being hurtful." That feeling is not caused by manipulation. Manipulation happens when someone tries to make you feel guilty about something that really isn't your fault. They try to engender a false sense of guilt by trying to make you feel responsible for both how they feel and for making them happier. This strategy is most effective when the manipulator is emotionally close to you, a friend or family member, for example. There are several techniques that are used to manipulate guilt.

The most common tactic is for another person to try to make you feel responsible for their unhappiness. You must ask yourself whether your actions (or inaction) are responsible for how that person feels? If they are, then feeling guilt is a reasonable response. However, if their unhappiness is not due to anything you have done, they may still try to provoke feelings of guilt to get you to do what they want. This is most effective if you are a people-pleaser who sees themselves as responsible for everyone's happiness. Guilt-trippers are very good at identifying and targeting people-pleasers. Take a step back and look at the situation. Are you responsible for that person's unhappiness? If not, will you choose to help them? If you do, that is fine, as long as you are certain that you aren't being manipulated by a false sense of guilt.

Another common tactic is using this phrase: *"Remember what I did for you!"* In this situation, the manipulator will refer to past instances where they helped you. This help may be real or imagined and, on the surface, this is a difficult tactic to resist. It seems perfectly reasonable that the person is reminding you of a past event and making it clear that they expect you to return the favor. But take a moment to think it through. Is what the person is claiming really true? Did they provide you with help or support when you needed it? People who use the manipulation of guilt to get what they want are often insecure and needy, and they don't generally make supportive friends, colleagues, or partners. So, if you consider the situation objectively, you may see that their claim lacks merit.

Even if someone has provided you with assistance in the past, you should question why they are referring to that. A person who truly gives you help for positive reasons does not do this in the expectation that you will do the same for them. Nor will they remind you of past help in order to get you to do what they want. If someone uses this technique, they are almost certainly trying to use your feelings of guilt to manipulate you.

Guilt manipulators may also use this tactic to try to deflect attention from something they have done by shifting the basis of the discussion. For example, imagine that you have come across a series of emails to and from your partner that are more than mildly flirtatious. You're angry, and you confront your partner. Instead of discussing the content of the e-mails, they claim to be outraged by this invasion of their privacy. They try to shift the guilt to you and in the process, deflect discussion of their own behavior.

Any time you find yourself confronted by a guilt-tripper, ask yourself a simple question: have you done anything to feel guilty for? In other words, have your actions or inaction cased that person's unhappiness? If you are directly responsible, then that person may be completely justified in telling you how they feel and expecting you to respond. If you are not responsible, but the person is still trying to make you feel guilty, perhaps you are dealing with a guilt-tripper. That situation doesn't mean that you can't offer them support, but it does mean that you can be on-guard against manipulation.

Emotional blackmail

Emotional blackmail is a term that most people have heard, but what does it mean? This phrase has been around since the 1940s[7], though it was popularized in the late 1990s by psychotherapist Susan Forward in her book *Emotional Blackmail: When the People in Your Life Use Fear, Obligation, and Guilt to Manipulate You*. In this book, Forward describes the use of what she calls FOG (fear, obligation, and guilt) to manipulate people within relationships. Emotional blackmail is now a widely accepted term used to describe the transactional dynamics of certain relationships.

Emotional blackmail involves another person using your own feelings to manipulate you. This tactic can be similar to the manipulation of guilt, but it uses other feelings too. It is called blackmail because it usually takes the form of a threat, with someone saying (or at least implying): *"Do what I want or suffer the consequences."* Forward describes four different forms that such threats may take.

> The **punisher's threat** is probably the most common and obvious form of emotional blackmail. Punishers use overt threats to get what they want. They may be aggressive, and their threat often takes the form of *"If you do X, I'll do Y."* The sanctions that punishers impose may include the withdrawal of physical affection, the "silent treatment," abandonment, or even

---

[7] *Emotional Blackmail Climate*, Journal of the National Association of Deans of Women, 1947.

physical violence. Punishers are the embodiment of the *"my way or the highway"* philosophy. They want a relationship that is entirely on their terms or no relationship at all. Punishers generally use explicit threats and fear of real or imagined consequences to get what they want: *"If you don't do what I want, I'll leave you."* Because it tends to be obvious, the punisher's threat is one of the easiest forms of emotional blackmail to recognize.

The **self-punisher's threat** is similar but uses a different basis to manipulate your feelings. Instead of relying on fear, the self-punisher invokes your sense of guilt to manipulate you. Like the punisher, the self-punisher uses statements based on *"If you do X, I'll do Y,"* but instead of threats intended to evoke fear, the consequences are portrayed as harmful to the manipulator. *"If you don't go to the party with me, I'll become depressed,"* or *"If you leave me, I'll kill myself."* The self-punisher often suffers from a lack of self-esteem, and they may truly believe that you are responsible for their happiness. They may refuse to take responsibility for their own lives. They may be needy. They will play on your sense of responsibility to get what they want. Self-punishers are desperate to take control of relationships, and they will resort to the most dramatic means to do this. Self-punishers are seldom subtle, and like punishers, they are usually easy to identify.

The **sufferer** is similar to the self-punisher, but rather than threatening consequences based on internal factors, they claim that unless you do what they want, they will be affected by negative external factors. For example, imagine that you see a friend flirting with someone who isn't their partner. The friend realizes that you have seen and uses the threat, "*If you tell my partner, it will ruin our relationship.*" Just like all the other forms of emotional blackmail, this manipulation seeks to transfer responsibility to you. In this example, it tries to make you feel responsible for the continuation of a relationship and for the happiness of the person involved. One thing that is notable about this form of emotional blackmail is that it can be difficult to identify. Punishers and self-punishers are easy to spot because they make overt threats. Sufferers may not openly say what they think. They may rely on body language or a withdrawal of affection to let you know how they feel. Sometimes, it seems that sufferers expect you to be able to read their minds, and they become angry and frustrated when you can't do this.

The **tantalizer** is the most subtle of all the emotional blackmailers. Rather than using the threat of negative feelings like fear and guilt to get what they want, this type of blackmailer uses vague promises of future rewards. They may seem to promise a perfect relationship, a dazzling career, or a reward that will provide emotional, financial, or physical gratification. They set a series of tests that you must pass if we are to receive the reward. The series of tests gets longer and longer, and the promised reward gets further and further away. Tantalizers don't deliver. They never have any intention of providing the reward they seem to be offering. This is simply a way of using your hope and expectation to get what they want.

It is important to be able to recognize the four main types of emotional blackmailer. However, you should not assume that all four are separate. There are no firm boundaries between these forms of blackmail, and a manipulative person may use all four forms of blackmail to get what they want. No matter which form is used, the process of emotional blackmail generally follows six distinct steps:

- **Demand**. There is something that the blackmailer wants. This goal may be intangible and emotional (more affection, increased love), or it may be concrete and physical (a new car, a workplace promotion).
- **Resistance**. The subject of the blackmail does not feel comfortable with providing what the blackmailer wants.
- **Pressure.** The blackmailer applies pressure to get what they want.
- **Threat.** The blackmailer uses fear or guilt, or in the case of the tantalizer, the promise of a reward, to increase the pressure on the subject.

- **Compliance.** The subject gives in and provides the blackmailer with what they want.
- **Repetition.** Having discovered that this technique gets them what they want, the blackmailer will use it again and again.

Blackmail is used to apply pressure to make you act in ways that make you feel uncomfortable and may even go against your core values. Because of this, giving in to emotional blackmail makes you feel bad about yourself and impacts your self-esteem and self-image. You must be on guard for the techniques used by emotional blackmailers. Once you learn to recognize them, they are easier to defend against.

Passive-aggressive behavior

Being assertive and using open emotional communication is not easy. Many people try to achieve their aims not by being overtly assertive, but by using indirectly aggressive behavior, hiding negative feelings beneath seemingly positive language. This strategy leads to a basic disconnect between how a person feels and what they say. The term *"passive-aggressive"* was first used during the Second World War to describe soldiers who would find ways not to carry out orders, though they would not directly refuse to obey.

People who display this behavior may have experienced childhoods where the expression of emotion was not encouraged or where any form of dissent was seen as a threat. They may simply learn this behavior as adults, discovering that it helps them to get what they want while avoiding direct confrontation. People may only be passive-aggressive in certain situations. For example, a person may behave this way at work but not within personal relationships.

People who suffer from this behavior often don't recognize it as a problem. They see it as avoiding conflict or hurting other people's feelings. They may justify it as a way of negating potential problems at work where a simple refusal to do something may have serious consequences. Everyone can behave this way sometimes. We have all been in a situation where we would like to say something, but we don't, often because we want to avoid conflict. However, if this becomes the standard way we respond to stress, then it can become a problem.

How can you identify a person who is being passive-aggressive? The most obvious sign is a clear disconnect between what the person is saying and the non-verbal cues they provide. *"No, I don't mind that you are late"* may be what the person is saying, but their obvious impatience and glances at their watch show that's not how they really feel. And when they add, *"This will make me late for my next meeting, but I suppose that will be all right,"* you can see that it really isn't all right at all. However, all forms of passive-aggressive behavior allow the user the luxury of *"plausible deniability."* If you confront them directly, they can deny that they are angry at all.

A classic sign of passive-aggression is leaving actions undone. Whether it's at work or home, the passive-aggressive person will rarely come right out and tell you they don't want to do something. Instead, they will seem to agree to do it. But somehow, that thing just never seems to get done. The passive-aggressive person will always have excuses as to why this is, so that if you confront them, they can claim that they really do intend to do that thing. Often, they will tell you that the task is almost done, but it never quite gets finished. This trait means that passive-aggressive people make infuriating employees, colleagues, and partners. Whatever you suggest, they will agree to. But they will find reasons not to do it without having to directly confront their own feelings of anger, hurt, or frustration.

One of the factors that makes this behavior so difficult to deal with is that the person suffering from it may not even be aware. Some passive-aggressive people have become so used to hiding negative feelings that they almost seem to have forgotten that they experience them. If challenged, a passive-aggressive person will almost always deny feeling, for example, anger, even when their body language and other non-verbal cues make it very evident that they are angry. How can you be certain that someone is being passive-aggressive?

One of the classic forms of this behavior is withdrawing contact. Or, as it's known in children, sulking. If you have done something the passive-aggressive person does not like, they may completely ignore you. This behavior can range from silence to a less obvious lack of eye contact and an "*accidental*" failure to greet you or include you in conversations. This latter approach is more popular because if challenged, the passive-aggressive person will be able to deny that they have been ignoring you at all.

Passive-aggressive people are also masters of the subtle insult. This is an attack on your weak point that is so disguised that, if necessary, it can be denied or even presented as a compliment. After all, what is wrong with saying: "*Hey, that looks good. Stripes are so slimming!*" Except that perhaps it is intended to draw attention to your weight as much as it is to be a real compliment. One of the most difficult aspects of dealing with a person who is passive-aggressive is that it is so difficult to confront them with what they are doing. All their actions are carefully designed to be deniable, and in many cases, they are not even fully aware of what they are doing.

But, just like the other behaviors described in this chapter, passive-aggressive behavior is ultimately about control. Specifically, it is about getting what you want without the stress of conflict or the honesty of assertiveness.

Toxic takers

The last type of behavior that you must guard against is the toxic- taker. This is the person who will take from you everything they can, simply because they feel entitled to do so. They will take your time and your energy, expect you to do them favors, and in turn they will give nothing but resentment and negativity.

The term *"toxic takers"* was first used by Organizational Psychologist and New York Times columnist Adam Grant[8]. Grant describes the three orientations of which we are all capable: givers, takers, and matchers. Givers provide support and encouragement without expecting anything in return. Matchers provide support but they expect to be supported in return. Takers seize opportunities for themselves, hoard scarce resources, and take all the credit for success and steal ideas. This creates a toxic atmosphere of distrust and competition. That is why they are known as us toxic takers.

Toxic takers exist in the workplace and elsewhere. Some people may be a toxic taker in one place and may act differently in a different environment. Toxic takers are a particular hazard for the unassertive. Toxic takers may be colleagues, siblings, friends, neighbors, or acquaintances. What they will have in common is a feeling of

---

[8] *Successful Givers, Toxic Takers, and the Life we Spend at Work.* On-line discussion between Adam Grant and *On Being* host Krista Tippet. https://onbeing.org/programs/adam-grant-successful-givers-toxic-takers-and-the-life-we-spend-at-work/ Original Air Date, October 2015.

entitlement, that they have a right to benefit from your expertise and the results of your hard work.

The toxic taker often presents as someone who is very aware of their own faults. They may seem endearingly bad at whatever they do. Their conversation is self-deprecating, focusing on their failures and inabilities. At first, that doesn't seem so bad. But then you begin to notice that they only want to talk about themselves, never about you. And you notice that they constantly ask for your help. When you give that help, they not only don't acknowledge it, but they also sometimes pass off what you have helped them to do as their own work.

Given even longer, you may become aware of something else. That toxic taker doesn't actually like you very much. They resent your seeming success, and they resent the fact that they need your help. Not only will they take everything you can give, but they may also even be working to influence what other people think about you. Toxic takers come in four distinct forms.

> The first type of a toxic taker is the person who only spends time with you when they want something. That person who spends time chatting at your desk at work but ignores you at social gatherings may be a toxic taker. Do they only ever come to you at work because they want help with the printer or to get ideas for their latest report? In a social setting, there may be nothing they want from you, so they won't bother to spend time with you.

The second type of toxic taker is the person who will reciprocate, but only if they are forced to. This person goes to lunch with you regularly, but you realize that it's always you who pays. You point this out, and the other person is forced to agree and pays. But in the future, you may find that their schedule has suddenly become too busy for them to find the time for lunch with you.

The third type of toxic taker will help you out, but they will want immediate recompense. Yes, they'll give you a lift home, but they will ask for cash to cover the additional fuel. This may even be a partner that will pick up the shopping you forgot, but they will want to receive half the cash immediately.

The fourth type of toxic taker is the most common. These are people who spend time with you and expect you to give them support and encouragement, but in return they will provide you with nothing. Sometimes, it seems that this type of person doesn't really know you at all. They certainly won't know when your birthday or anniversary is, and they'll be surprised when you tell them about those new evening classes you are attending (Despite the fact that you told them all about it and how excited and nervous you were the last time you spoke). This type of toxic taker can be difficult to spot. It may only be when you realize that they really don't listen to anything you say that you understand that they don't know you at all and care even less.

All toxic takers are a problem. They take your time, energy, and support, and they give nothing in return.

Part 2: How to Increase Your Assertiveness

In the first part of this book, we explained in detail how your own beliefs and those of the people you spend time with can stop you from being assertive. As you were reading, hopefully you have identified how these beliefs are impacting your life.

Now, it's time to begin talking about the steps you can take to address these problems. It's time for you to learn how to become assertive.

Chapter 5: What You Need to Know About Being Assertive

Take an assertiveness test

It is helpful to understand what level of assertiveness you are starting from. To assess this, take the short test below. In each case, you are presented with a scenario. Choose response "a", "b", or "c" as most accurately representing your typical reaction. Write down your answers.

1) You leave a shop and realize that the amount of change you got back is wrong. Do you:
   a) Just ignore it. The shop was busy. The server probably made a mistake, and it wasn't a great deal of money anyway.
   b) Go back into the shop, demand to speak with the manager, and tell them that the server cheated you.
   c) Go back into the shop, talk to the server, and point out that they have made a mistake.
2) You take your car to the garage for repairs. You are given an estimate of the cost but when you return, the bill includes additional charges for extra work. Do you:
   a) Pay the bill without commenting on the extra work.
   b) Refuse to pay the bill.
   c) Point out that this amount is more than the agreed price and ask the manager to explain the extra work.

3) You are watching an interesting television show. Your partner/friend/roommate comes in and asks you for help. Do you:
   a) Turn off the television and immediately help.
   b) Refuse to help because you're watching the show.
   c) Explain that you're watching the show and ask if you can help after it's finished.
4) A friend is visiting. They stay longer than expected, preventing you from completing an important task. Do you:
   a) Say nothing and hope that you can find some extra time to finish the task when they leave.
   b) Tell the friend you have something to do and ask them to leave so you can complete your task.
   c) Explain that there is something you need to do and ask if perhaps you could get back together at a better time?
5) You invite a friend to dinner. They don't arrive and don't call. Do you:
   a) Say nothing, but next time that friend asks you to dinner, accept the invitation but don't go.
   b) Berate your friend and criticize them in the presence of other people.
   c) Call the friend and ask them if they have a problem.
6) You are involved in a discussion about a work project. A colleague asks a question about your contribution. You don't know the answer. Do you:
   a) Make up an answer that sounds plausible and that no one will recognize as a lie.

b) Deflect the question by asking the colleague a question you know they will find difficult or impossible to answer.

c) Admit that you don't know the answer but tell the colleague that you will find out and get back to them.

7) You feel that someone doesn't like you, but you can't think of any reason for this. Do you:

a) Worry, but don't say anything in case you offend the person.

b) Think of ways of getting back at the person.

c) Confront the person by asking them if there is a problem.

In each case "a" represents a passive response, "b" an aggressive response, and c"" represents assertive behavior. In any given situation, people generally react in one of these three ways. You can see that the passive responses don't provide solutions and may leave you feeling angry and frustrated. The aggressive responses may get short-term results, but they will also leave other people feeling resentful and angry. The assertive responses are focused on looking for a solution while maintaining your rights and protecting your feelings.

As you work through this part of the book, your responses should start to change. Perhaps when you have begun to put into practice some of the strategies to become more assertive, you may want to come back and look at this test again to see if your responses have changed.

Assertiveness is a choice

You determine how you respond to problems. Passive people often feel that they have no choice, and they tell themselves that they are forced into acting as they do. In truth, being passive is a choice. Saying nothing is a choice. Accepting bullying is a choice. Always doing what other people say is a choice. The problem for passive people is that they have a skewed view of the consequences of their actions.

They tell themselves that it's best not to say what they think because if they do, people may not like them. They tell themselves that it is best not to stand up to their boss because otherwise, they might lose their job. They tell themselves it is best to go along with what their partner wants because otherwise the relationship might end. These perceptions are not true. This is just how passive persons see the world and these perceptions are the reasons for the choices that passive people make.

Aggressive people also make choices. They have discovered that aggression provides a way of covering insecurity and self-doubt and aggression is a way of taking control. They continue with their bullying, overbearing behavior because they cannot see any other way of getting what they want.

If you can recognize aggression and passivity, hopefully you can see that the third alternative, assertiveness, is the best approach for you and others. But, just like passivity and aggression, assertiveness is something you learn.

Self-confidence and assertiveness

There is a clear and direct link between self-confidence and the ability to be assertive. Passive people often suffer from a lack of self-confidence and seek to bolster this deficiency by turning into people-pleasers. Becoming more assertive will help boost your self-confidence but becoming assertive requires self-confidence. How can you boost your self-confidence to get started? We will provide detailed strategies later for boosting your self-confidence, but meanwhile, here are some tips:

Don't compare yourself to other people. Comparing yourself to friends, colleagues, or family members is not healthy. It's all too easy to feel inadequate and envious. A 2018 study[9] found a direct link between envy and self-confidence. When you find yourself feeling like a failure because you aren't as attractive/successful/wealthy as other people, stop! Life isn't a race. You aren't in competition with those people, and their attainments do not make you a failure. You have many accomplishments to be proud of. Focus on those achievements and keep working towards your personal goals.

Learn self-compassion. Don't beat yourself up if you make a mistake or you fail to achieve

---

[9] Vrabel JK, Zeigler-Hill V, Southard AC. *Self-esteem and envy: Is state self-esteem instability associated with the benign and malicious forms of envy?* Personality and Individual Differences, 2018.

something. Failures are opportunities for learning and the only people who never fail are those who never try anything. Instead, treat yourself with kindness and understanding, just as you would if you were dealing with another person.

Celebrate your successes. It's all too easy to fall into the trap of focusing on our failures and not noticing our many successes. Make a conscious effort to take note of activities you do well. Give yourself a pat on the back. Recognize what you are good at.

Try something new. Our brains thrive on the challenge of dealing with new things, but often, fear holds us back. Try to try something you find scary. When you succeed, you will be amazed at how much more confident you feel.

That last point is very important in the context of assertiveness. For many people, the idea of learning a new skill makes them very nervous. When you learn the skills, you need to be assertive, you will discover just how much that boosts your self-confidence.

You can also boost your self-confidence and strength to face adversity by developing mental toughness. By building mental resilience you will also improve your self-confidence and courage to face adversity. You will find out at the end of this book how mental toughness can help you build confidence and accomplish goals like being more confident and confronting the challenges life can throw at you.

We all have needs, psychological and physical. Not all of our needs can be fulfilled completely, all the time. That realization is part of the cost of living within a society. We must sometimes set aside our own needs in order to meet the greater needs of others. That kind of compromise is normal and natural.

Needs are important. They are not self-indulgent or simply dreams that we know will never come true. They are your core values, and if they are consistently unfulfilled, you may become frustrated, dissatisfied, and even depressed. It is all too easy to lose sight of your own needs, particularly if you spend your time focused on the needs of others.

Needs are complex and different for everyone. However, motivational speaker and author Tony Robbins has identified six core needs that everyone shares:

> **Certainty** is concerned with consistency, stability, security, safety, and control. You need to have structure within your life to give you the reassurance that you understand what the future is likely to bring.

> **Variety** notes that too much certainty actually creates boredom. So, within an overall context of certainty, you do need change, spontaneity, and difference.

> **Significance** is the need to feel respected, valued, honored, and validated by other people. This can be both in our personal and professional lives.

Connection is the need we all have to develop relationships that involve intimacy and love.

Growth is about positive change, whether that is physical, emotional, intellectual, or spiritual. We all need to feel that we are moving forward, that we are improving.

Contribution is the need to do good, to help others, and to make the world a better place in some way.

Take the time to look at these headings and think about your own needs. Are there areas in which you feel unfulfilled?

Assertiveness will give you the techniques to help fulfill your needs. But first, you need to clearly understand what those needs are.

The importance of assertive communication

Communication is at the heart of assertiveness. After all, you cannot expect people to behave in ways that meet your needs if you can't tell them what these needs are. People are not mind-readers. If you are not happy, the only way you can change this situation is to tell people what is causing your unhappiness and what you want them to do to change that.

Behavioral Communication[10] is a psychological construct that looks at people's day-to-day communication through the lens of different types of behavior. Specifically, it describes most normal communication as falling within one of the four following headings:

> **Aggressive communication** involves the aggressor deliberately setting out to hurt someone. This may be unplanned, and it may involve intimidation and bullying. Aggressive communicators generally lack empathy, see most situations in terms of winning or losing, seek confrontation, and do not listen to others.

> **Passive communication** often involves saying nothing at all, or certainly not anything that other people might find upsetting or challenging. Passive communicators rarely say what they really think, and they generally avoid making

---

[10] Ivanov, M., & Werner, P. D. *Behavioral communication: Individual differences in communication style.* Personality and Individual Differences (2010),

decisions and doing or saying anything that might result in any level of confrontation.

Passive-aggressive communication seems passive on the surface, but it is generally used as a mask for hostility and aggression. People using this communication style will employ sarcasm, hyperbole, and sulking.

Assertive communication is about appropriately expressing your needs and feelings while respecting the same things in other people. The assertive communicator is direct without deliberately provoking confrontation.

The notable point about these four styles of communication is that only assertive communication is open and honest. Passive and passive-aggressive communicators will rarely say what they really think, and aggressive communicators are not interested in genuine communication. Instead, they see most human interaction as an opportunity to win at the expense of other people.

Ask yourself, which of these communication styles would you rather deal with? It would be surprising if your answer were anything but the assertive communicator. Other people will feel the same and as you become more assertive, you will also become an assertive communicator. You will become the kind of person others want to communicate with.

The dos and don'ts of becoming assertive

Becoming assertive will transform your life. The ability to say what you want and to enforce your right to be happy are huge changes. However, before we begin talking about how to make those adjustments, here are four points that you must remember as you begin to use your new abilities:

> **Do choose your words carefully.** When you become assertive, you will be presenting yourself in a different way, and that will make people scrutinize what you say. You do not want to appear rude or aggressive. If you have a forthcoming meeting or discussion where you intend to assert yourself, think carefully about what you are going to say. You may even want to write this down so that you can examine it carefully. The form of words you choose is important, and this is especially significant when you first begin to practice being assertive.

> **Do listen.** Becoming assertive is mainly a communications skill but remember that communication has two sides: Speaking and listening. Make sure you really listen to what other people say and give weight to their views and feelings. That does not mean that you have to back down but achieving a balance between your needs and those of others may require compromise.

Don't take it personally. Sometimes, even when you do everything right, not everyone will be happy. That's understandable. If you are overly passive, up to now, other people have been able to treat you as they wish. Suddenly, you will be able to stand up for yourself and say how you feel and what you want. That's going to be a surprise at first, and some people aren't going to like it. They may react by being sarcastic, critical, or even rude. Learn to ignore this type of comment and move on.

Don't become arrogant. When you discover that your new assertiveness skills really work, you may begin to feel superior. However, take care to continue to treat others with respect and kindness and to remain humble. No matter how much you discover and grow, there is always more to learn.

Dealing with harmful beliefs

In Chapter 3, we looked at harmful beliefs that undermine your self-image and self-esteem. Most of us emerge from childhood with one or more beliefs that hold us back. You should have been able to identify the harmful beliefs that affect you. Now it's time to do something about them.

One of the most common and effective methods for dealing with harmful beliefs is to use the techniques of cognitive behavioral therapy (CBT). CBT practitioners teach that maladaptive thoughts and beliefs cause feelings of sadness and depression. Changing the way that you think changes the way that you feel. If you feel more positive, it is much easier to be confident and assertive.

You have already identified the beliefs that are causing you to act in unhelpful ways. Many CBT practitioners use a simple acronym to describe the approach to changing those beliefs: BLUE. This stands for:

> **Blaming yourself**. This part of maladaptive thinking involves feeling responsible for circumstances over which you have no control. It often involves feeling responsible for other people's happiness. Accepting responsibility for your own actions is commendable and mature. Feeling guilty about situations that you are not responsible for is harmful to you and completely ineffective. When you feel guilty about something, you must learn to look objectively at what it is that is making you feel that way. Is something that you have done, or not done, the cause of the situation? For example, a friend or

partner is clearly unhappy. Unless you are the direct cause of that unhappiness, you must not blame yourself for how the other person is feeling, and you must not feel responsible for somehow distracting them from their unhappiness. Empathy and compassion are always appropriate, and these feelings combined with assertiveness skills will allow you to support and guide a person who is unhappy. Blaming yourself inappropriately is counter-productive and something you must learn to identify and reject.

Looking for bad news. Unfortunately, we all tend to dwell unduly on negative information. Imagine you have given a presentation at work on a project you are leading. Nine of the 10 people present are positive about your report. One person is mildly critical and doubtful. How do you feel after the presentation? Chances are that you focus on the negative comment and completely disregard all the positive comments. This reaction is normal and natural, but it is something you must be aware of and guard against. Now try to imagine that someone you care about had given that presentation. They were upset by the negative comment. What would you say to them? Of course, you would point out that the majority of people present were positive and supportive and that overall, the presentation was a success. You must learn to look at your own experiences and reactions as if they apply to someone else.

This approach helps to be objective. You must also make a conscious effort to direct your thinking towards the positive. In virtually every situation, there is good news if you look for it. Even a complete failure provides invaluable opportunities for learning and for avoiding the same mistake in future.

Unhappy guessing. We all spend a great deal of time trying to guess what will happen in the future. However, sometimes we fall into patterns of thinking that make us expect the worst. Imagine that you have organized a trip to a restaurant for a group of friends. What will happen if you spend the days before thinking: "*I just know this is going to be a disaster!*" This behavior is completely unproductive, and it means that when you finally arrive for the meal, you will already be feeling negative and pessimistic. That is not a good frame of mind in which to approach the evening. Now think about what would happen if you spent the days before thinking: "*This is going to be the best meal ever!*". Not only will you avoid several days of unnecessary and unproductive anxiety, but you will approach the event in a positive frame of mind. The future will always be uncertain. Doing everything you can to make the future positive is sensible and productive. Assuming that everything will turn out badly simply generates anxiety and changes nothing. Teach yourself to change what you can but not to always assume a negative outcome.

Exaggeratedly negative. *"I hate my life!"* is the kind of statement we associate with unhappy teenagers, but in truth, we all sometimes make the error of seeing situations as being worse than they really are. This kind of thinking makes everything look negative and removes hope and optimism. If you find yourself having this kind of thought, imagine your response if someone else made this statement. Consider how you would point out the positives and put the negatives in context.

Now, let's go back to the harmful beliefs we discussed in Chapter 3 and see how we can turn those "BLUE" beliefs into true beliefs.

The need to please

> B – "It's my fault if my partner/friend/colleague isn't happy."

> L – "If I don't make them happy, they won't like me."

> U – "It must be something I have done."

> E – "If I don't make them happy, they won't want to spend time with me."

> True belief: Empathy and compassion are good, but it is right to also consider my own needs and feelings. We are all responsible for our own

happiness, and it isn't your responsibility to make everyone else happy.

Insecurity and self-doubt

B – "I'm so stupid/fat/unattractive!"

L – "My failings mean that no one will ever love me."

U – "I never get anything right."

E – "Why would anyone want to spend time with me?"

True belief: You are worthy of love and respect, just as you are. You may have failings. Everyone does. But you also have positive attributes that make you attractive, interesting, and worthy of respect.

The need to be good

B – "Unless I please other people, no one will like me."

L – "Thinking about my own needs and feelings is selfish."

U – "If I don't behave in a particular way, I won't be popular."

E – "If I am selfish, no one will care about me."

True belief: You have a right to be happy. You do not have a responsibility to please other people.

Always doing what other people want and expect will not bring respect and love.

Fear of confrontation and submission

B – "If I say that, my partner/friend/colleague will be unhappy."

L – "If there is an argument, I will look bad."

U – "I shouldn't say that because it may make someone unhappy."

E – "If I say what I really think, people will feel that I'm selfish."

True belief: Your life goals and aims will never be identical to those of another person. That means that some level of confrontation is inevitable as you find solutions that provide benefit to everyone. Avoiding all confrontation by always submitting to other people's needs will not provide love and respect.

Being assertive is nasty!

B – "If I say what I really feel, no one will like me."

L – "It's just rude to tell other people how I feel."

U – "If I keep quiet, it will all be OK."

E – "No one will want to listen to me."

True belief: You have a right to say how you feel and tell other people what they can do to change that. Of course, you must not trample on other people's feelings, and you must find ways of expressing what you want that are not offensive or aggressive.

It's not my fault!

This last harmful belief is slightly different. In this case, the "B" in BLUE stands for *"Blaming others,"* but the approach is still valid.

> B – "If my partner/friend/colleague would just act differently, I would be happy."
>
> L – "Other people are always making me unhappy."
>
> U – "I will never be happy because no one cares."
>
> E – "No one wants to make me happy."

True belief: You are responsible for your own happiness. No one else has the ability to change your happiness, nor are they responsible for it.

Go through the harmful beliefs you identified in Chapter 3. Apply the BLUE technique to them and try to arrive at a true belief. Simply looking in detail at your own beliefs reduces their effect on your thinking and helps you to recognize negative and harmful thoughts.

Hardships, challenges, and obstacles in your life can all lead to harmful thoughts. These difficulties will call for self-doubts and it can be difficult to change your views and become assertive if you are not mentally tough and resilient. You can learn more about developing mental toughness at the end of this book

Dealing with emotional blackmail

Emotional blackmailers use feelings of fear, guilt, and obligation to manipulate you into doing what they want. However, their manipulation means that they don't use real and justified feelings. Instead, they try to make you feel these emotions when they are not appropriate. The key to dealing with this form of manipulation is to ask yourself a simple question about what it is that they want you to do:

"Am I asserting my own free will or acting because I feel fear, guilt, or obligation?"

This is not an easy question to answer. First, it means really thinking about your own feelings. This may involve facing the fact that you feel fear or guilt. Consider why you are feeling this way. Have you done something that should make you feel fear or guilt? Do you really owe the other person an obligation, perhaps because of help they have given you in the past? Or is the manipulator trying to evoke these feelings when they have no real basis?

The most important point about emotional blackmail is that it uses emotions to get you to do what the manipulator wants. These are feelings evoked only through the manipulation. If you can recognize that, then it will lessen their impact on you. Of course, you still need to confront the manipulator. That is something that we will cover in a later chapter where we provide strategies for saying *"No."*

Dealing with toxic takers

When you have identified someone in your life as a toxic taker, there are two techniques you can use to effectively deal with them.

The toxic taker always comes to you with a problem, and they expect you to help deal with it. The first method involves listening when they tell you about the problem and offering sympathy. Nothing else. No time, advice, money, or any other kind of help at all. Simply respond to their recounting of the problem with something along the lines of *"That sounds really terrible. How awful for you."* Responding in that way is much harder than it sounds. You may be conditioned to offer help when someone tells you they have a problem. However, with toxic takers, doing so will simply lead to them asking for more and more. You must be steadfast in offering nothing but sympathy.

The toxic taker will be surprised. After all, they have become used to you providing them with what they want. So, they will probably try again. Stay strong. Repeat their feelings back to them to show that you have listened. But don't offer to help. They may then move on to a direct appeal for help, perhaps backed-up by emotional blackmail. You already know how to deal with this, and later, we'll tell you how to specifically say *"No"* in any circumstances. Faced with a refusal to cooperate, the toxic taker will quickly move on to another person who is easier to manipulate.

Another strategy to use with toxic takers is to listen to their tale of woe and then respond with a story about hardships you are facing. No toxic taker wants competition, and you will notice that they find it hard to listen to your story and they will not offer any type of help. Faced with this sort of response, most toxic takers will simply look elsewhere for a victim.

True toxic takers will quickly disappear from your life when you employ these techniques. People who are friends, but who may have become used to taking advantage of you, will not. But they will readjust to the new form of the relationship.

Chapter 7: Learning to Say *"No"*

Saying *"No"* is something many of us find difficult. Whether this hesitancy is in response to a request for help or an invite to an event we really don't want to attend, we are afraid that a refusal will offend the person asking. However, learning to say *"No"* is one of the basic skills involved in becoming assertive. In Part 3, we will provide detailed strategies for saying *"No"* with grace and respect. First, let's talk about why saying *"No"* is so difficult and yet important.

Why we're afraid to say *"No"*

One of the hardest words to say is *"No."* Even when we recognize that this may be the best thing to say, we find ourselves in situations where we say *"Yes"* instead. But just why is it that we find this so hard to say? There are a number of reasons, so let's look at those in some detail.

Saying *"Yes"* boosts our self-esteem. It can make us feel useful, needed, and valued. Conversely, we fear that saying *"No"* may have the opposite effect. We all like to feel valued and needed. However, we can become so embedded in behaviors designed to engender these feelings in others that we end up neglecting our own feelings and needs. Saying *"No"* for example, to a request for help, can initially dent our self-esteem. But, if we are doing this in order to reclaim time, energy or other resources for ourselves, this feeling will soon pass. Helping others is good. But becoming so addicted to this that you are incapable of saying *"No"* is not.

We want people to like us and disappointing them by saying *"No"* has an effect on how they feel about us.

There is no way around this. If you constantly say "*Yes*" to everything, people will soon begin to take this for granted and it won't lead to them liking or respecting you. If you can condition yourself to consider each request for help objectively and to say "*Yes*" only where it is truly appropriate, you will find that people appreciate that much more than the continuous "*Yes*" they get from a people-pleaser.

Probably the most common reason for not saying "*No*" is a fear of confrontation. If you say "*No,*" people may get emotional. They may even get angry or try to bully you, especially if they are used to your always saying "*Yes.*" Again, there is no way of avoiding some level of confrontation if you are going to learn to assert yourself by saying "*No.*" However, we will provide techniques for lessening emotional reactions.

Finally, we may fear missing out on opportunities when we say "*No.*" For example, if you are offered the chance to take on a new project at work, you may be concerned that you might miss out on promotion if you refuse. However, you only have so much time and energy available. Every time you say "*Yes*" to something, that will use more of your resources. And that will leave you less able to take on more beneficial new opportunities. It is important that you assess new opportunities and look at what they offer. Don't just accept everything that comes along because you are afraid of missing out.

Why learning to say *"No"* is healthy

Saying *"Yes"* when you really want to say *"No"* is something that most of us have done, but it's not good for us or the other people we are involved with. When someone asks us for a favor or invites to an event, when we say *"Yes"* but don't really mean it, we are essentially lying. That's bad for your self-esteem, it creates resentment, and it may even prompt you to act passive-aggressively by pretending to forget about what you promised to do.

In relationships, honesty and respect are fundamental. If you lie, you are undermining the relationship and showing a lack of respect for the other person. Conversely, if you can learn to say *"No"* when that is what you mean, that shows respect for the other person and honesty within the relationship.

Learning to say *"No"* also helps to set personal boundaries, limits that clearly define what you will and won't do. These help others to understand what you want and increase mutual respect within any relationship. Saying *"No"* to an action that you don't want to do also frees up your time and energy to say *"Yes"* to actions that you do want to do.

Finally, saying *"No"* is about looking after yourself. It is a fundamental part of accepting and making clear to others that you have feelings and needs and that these are important to you. We have discussed previously how looking after yourself is a critical element of becoming a balanced and confident person. Learning to express how

you feel is a central part of this personal development
and saying *"No"* when that's what you mean is a core skill.

"I can't" vs. "I won't"

When you are faced with a situation where you are asked to do something and you don't want to do it, but you are nervous about saying "*No,*" it may be tempting to use excuses to justify your refusal. In other words, to respond to that request by saying "*I can't*" rather than "*I won't.*" For example, a friend asks for help moving to a new apartment. You just don't have the energy to carry boxes up and down stairs, and you already have plans for "*me*" time at the weekend. However, instead of telling your friend this, you make up an excuse such as "*I have to take my sister to the hospital.*"

You feel that sounds more significant and acceptable than just explaining that you're tired and you need some down time. It's still a lie. You are not treating the relationship as important enough to justify honesty, and you are undermining your own self-esteem by feeling pressured into being untruthful. Even worse, if the friend believes your excuse, they may suggest doing it the next weekend or during an evening. What do you do then? Do you create another fictitious excuse or find yourself forced to do something you don't want to?

Saying *"No"* by explaining honestly why you won't do something is tough. But it is always going to be better for you and the relationship than saying "*I can't*" and inventing an excuse.

Chapter 8: Setting Boundaries

Why personal boundaries matter

Personal boundaries are the limits you set for what you will and will not do and what behavior you find acceptable in others. Setting these boundaries is an important part of assertiveness, but like the other elements of this skill, it can seem difficult. We all want to seem *"agreeable,"* willing to go along with what other people want because we believe that will make us liked and socially accepted. Surprisingly, a number of studies seem to show that is not so.

A report on a 2015 study published in the *Personality and Social Psychology Review*[11] analyzed participant reactions in games that featured social dilemmas and the need for bargaining. Participants disliked selfish players, which was unsurprising. However, the report found that agreeable players, those who didn't care if they won or lost were equally disliked. Discussion seemed to show that these players made others feel bad about themselves but that they were also seen as rule-breakers, even though the rules they broke were those that encouraged competition and confrontation.

A combined study in 2011 by the University of Notre Dame, Cornell University, and the University of Western

---

[11] Kun Zhao, Luke D Smillie, *The Role of Interpersonal Traits in Social Decision Making: Exploring Sources of Behavioral Heterogeneity in Economic Games*, August 2015, Personality and Social Psychology Review

Ontario[12] made it even more evident that being agreeable is not a positive career move. The study revealed that men classed as *"disagreeable"* earned, on average, 18% more than those who were classed as *"agreeable."* Men who were described as disagreeable were also often described as being effective negotiators and better managers. Even amongst women, where being seen as *"agreeable"* is a more recognized social norm, disagreeable females earned 5% more than their agreeable counterparts.

---

[12] Timothy A Judge, Beth A. Livingston, Charlice Hurst, *Do Nice Guys-and Gals-Really Finish Last? The Joint Effects of Sex and Agreeableness on Income,* Journal of Personality and Social Psychology, November 2011.

Choosing your boundaries

The boundaries you establish will include both your physical and emotional space. However, here we are concerned only with emotional boundaries. These represent the limits for how far you allow other people to enter your emotional space. How can you identify your limits? That's really fairly simple: If you are with someone who is making you feel uncomfortable, they are probably breaching your comfortable emotional limits.

To understand where those personal boundaries lie, take the time to think about your core values, the ideals, and actions that matter to you. Not the actions you take to please other people or because you feel that you are expected to do them. We are so used to adopting other people's needs and feelings into our own that it can be hard to remember what matters to us. For example, it may be that friendships are really important to you but you have one friend who regularly indulges in malicious gossip about other friends. Their behavior makes you feel uncomfortable, but you don't want to upset the gossiping friend by saying how you feel.

Boundaries are personal, and they will be different for everyone. Think them through and you will almost certainly find a disconnect between what is happening and your core values. That's when you need to set a clear boundary.

Enforcing your boundaries

Once you understand what your boundaries are, you can begin enforcing them. You have the right to defend your emotional personal space. However, remember that you can only change what you do, not what others do. If we go back to the example of the gossiping friend, you really don't have the right or responsibility to tell that friend to give up malicious gossip. That isn't up to you. Instead, you can firmly tell that friend that you don't care to hear that language and ask them to desist.

You may be nervous about the reaction you will get to setting such boundaries. Some people will react in an angry way. They may claim that you're being judgmental or unfair. You are not criticizing them or telling them to change your behavior in general. You are telling them that what they are doing makes you feel uncomfortable, and you are only asking them to stop doing it in your presence. Remember that being seen as disagreeable does not mean that people won't like or respect you. While the short-term reaction to your enforcement of boundaries may be negative, in the long term, doing this will generally make the relationship stronger because it will be more authentic and based on honesty.

Setting boundaries is an act of assertiveness. It can seem frightening. But there is no alternative. You must tell people when they are making you uncomfortable and why: You cannot expect them to guess. When you do this, it can be incredibly liberating and empowering.

Chapter 9: Do you want to be more assertive?

Making the choice to become more assertive

You now understand that being unassertive is a problem. In your personal and work life, it can make you ineffective, and it can also make you feel anxious, stressed, and unconfident. However, being passive isn't something innate that you just have to put up with. You can choose to become assertive. Only you can make that choice and only you can make that happen. Before we go any further, you need to ask yourself two important questions:

- Do you want to become more assertive?
- Are you prepared to put in the time and effort to become more assertive?

These are fundamental questions. If you can't answer *"Yes"* to both without reservations, you are probably wasting your time. Perhaps you need to go back through this book to see why being unassertive is hurting you, other people, and your relationships with them? Or perhaps you just need to accept that you will always be passive, trodden on and that you will never have the space or opportunity to look after your own needs and feelings?

What do you choose?

Assertiveness isn't all or nothing

This book provides an understanding of what a lack of assertiveness means and how to deal with that. It provides practical strategies for becoming more assertive. But you aren't going to put this book down, take a deep breath and suddenly become assertive in everything you do. Sadly, life just isn't that simple.

Begin by thinking about where your lack of assertiveness is hurting you most.

Think about areas in which becoming more assertive will bring you the most benefit.

Those are important targets to be aware of, but don't rush to start tackling the most difficult and stressful situations first. Even when you believe in your right to assert your own feelings and needs you will need to gradually build your skills and confidence. You will rehearse what you are going to do and say before you apply these techniques in the real world.

It's going to take time. You cannot become assertive overnight. You will be taking it step-by-step and building your confidence and your skills incrementally. However, each small step provides benefits. Learning to assert yourself, even in small ways, is liberating and empowering. As you become confident with the first small steps, you can extend your use of assertiveness techniques into other areas of your life.

Assertiveness isn't something you can do in a single session. It's a journey of transformation. And each journey begins with a single step.

How long will it take?

Your current passivity is something that you have learned. It is a set of behaviors that you have used for so long that they have become habitual and largely instinctual. You react to potential confrontation by doing whatever is necessary to avoid it, even though you aren't aware of this habit.

That behavior is going to change. You are going to be building a new set of behaviors that will become habitual responses. These changes will take time, though perhaps not as long as you may think. Many studies have been conducted to determine how long it takes for new behaviors to become habits, and there is still no universally agreed period. The timeframe depends on you and your circumstances. However, most estimates suggest that if you establish a new behavior and maintain it for between 30 and 90 days, it will become habitual.

Just think about that for a moment. If you can make a conscious effort to undertake new assertive behaviors for at least 90 days, they will become habits. You won't have to think about them. They will become automatic, positive responses. Focus on that thought as you set out to implement these new behaviors.

Listening to your wise advocate

In the seminal self-help book, *You Are Not Your Brain*[13], psychiatrists Jeffrey Schwartz and Rebecca Gladding describe a useful strategy for dealing with negative self-esteem and a lack of self-confidence. They call this the *"wise advocate."* This approach involves visualizing a person that you respect. It can be a real person, a family member, a friend, someone you know (or have known), or even a historical figure whose accomplishments you admire. It can even be a fictitious character. It really does not matter who this person is so long as:

- You can visualize them clearly to the extent of imagining conversations with that person,
- You must be able to visualize them as being wise, compassionate, kind, supportive, and they must genuinely care and want the best for you.

In other words, the wise advocate must be a person whose advice you would welcome and trust. If you find yourself in a situation where you are uncertain what to do, or struggle to find the confidence to do something , imagine describing that situation to your wise advocate.

This may sound overly simplified, but it is actually built on sound psychological principles. Imagining talking to your wise advocate helps gain a broader view of any situation and to move beyond the immediate emotions that may

---

[13] Schwartz, Jeffrey M, and Gladding, Rebecca. *You Are Not Your Brain: The 4-Step Solution for Changing Bad Habits, Ending Unhealthy Thinking, and Taking Control of Your Life*. Avery, 2011.

be confusing you. Best of all, the guidance from this wise advocate will always be positive and in your best interests.

Imagine your own wise advocate. Take the time to visualize them intensely and in detail. When you find yourself struggling with issues of self-confidence or you aren't sure what you should do, ask your wise advocate for advice. Often, this strategy will help you determine what to do and to find the assurance to do it.

Positive thinking

Positive thinking is an attitude that focuses on good outcomes. It is about acting because you anticipate happiness and success, not because you fear failure. Many motivational and self-help approaches stress the importance of positive thinking. Your thoughts dictate your actions. If your thoughts are positive, your actions will be, too. This behavior is far more likely to lead to success.

Positive thinking is particularly important for creating goals. Why do you want to become more assertive? What are your assertiveness goals? To be most effective, these must be positive.

For example, if your goal is to become more assertive at work, goals like *"I want to become more effective in my job"* or *"I want that promotion so I can use my skills better"* are positive. *"I want to make fewer mistakes at work"* or *"I don't want to lose my job"* are not. *"I want to improve my negotiating skills"* is a positive goal. *"I want to be better than X-person."* is not. Positive goals are about you. You have the ability and responsibility to change yourself. Comparing yourself to others or being focused on beating someone else undermines that focus.

Positive thinking is also about celebrating progress. At first, you will probably be asserting yourself in relatively small ways. These steps are not trivial. Recognize them and give yourself a pat on the back for every success. Treat yourself when you accomplish a goal. Recognizing when you succeed is as important, or perhaps even more important, than accepting when you fail. We all tend to castigate ourselves for failures while disregarding successes. Every success is a step on the way towards a better life.

Just like any other skill, positive thinking is something you learn to do. Take the time to look at what you have achieved. Teach yourself to look for positives in every situation, not to brood about failures. Acknowledge success and build on the confidence that comes from it.

And to stay on track with learning to think positive, change your mindset and achieve the goals you set, you will need to be resilient and mentally strong enough to not be hindered by the any challenges you might encounter. Learn more about developing mental toughness at the end of this book.

Empathy and sympathy

Empathy is an important part of good communication. However, these is some confusion about precisely what this word means and how is it different from, for example, sympathy.

The word *"empathy"* was first used in the early 20th century. It is a translation of a German term *"Einfhlung"* (feeling with), and it was introduced by British psychologist Edward Titchener. Most psychologists use the term empathy to mean the ability to imagine yourself in someone else's situation to understand their emotions. In the late 1950s, psychologist Carl Rogers was the first to suggest that empathy was an essential element of effective communication. Since then, many studies have confirmed this theory.

An empathetic person is able to see situations from another person's perspective. Although the two words are often used synonymously, empathy is different from sympathy. Sympathy is feeling *for* another person, as opposed to empathy, which is feeling *with* another person. In other words, sympathy is closer to feeling sorry for another person while empathy means understanding why they are experiencing certain feelings.

There are three elements to empathy:

- You must have a deep understanding of the other person's feelings.

- You must be able to understand what behaviors or situations have caused the other person's feelings.
- You must be able to let the other person know that you understand their feelings and what has caused them.

 Empathy is crucial to effective communication, and communication is central to assertiveness. Work on developing your empathy. Trying to understand why other people feel the way they do can help you to better understand where your own feelings come from. Some psychologists rate empathy as one of the elements of true psychological maturity.

Learning to listen

There is a fundamental difference between listening and hearing. Some studies suggest that as much as 75% of what we hear is almost immediately forgotten, ignored, or misunderstood. Part of learning to become assertive is understanding what other people want. This process involves *listening* to them. Not just hearing what they say, but really comprehending and letting the speaker know that you are doing this.

There are three critical skills involved in listening. These are:

> **Attending.** This is the nonverbal communication you provide to the speaker to confirm that you are listening. It involves body posture, eye contact, and giving undivided attention to what they are saying. Nothing makes it clearer that you are not listening than allowing your gaze to roam while the other person is talking or worse still, checking your phone or emails. If you want to show someone that you are really listening to them, face them, maintain eye contact, and don't allow your attention to wander.

> **Following.** Demonstrating this skill means not hijacking the conversation to suit your own agenda. Instead of interrupting with your own story, encourage the speaker to continue with cues like *"That's interesting, tell me more…"* or *"I didn't know that!"* Use open questions to encourage the speaker to tell you more.

Reflecting. People using the reflecting skill make comments that restate the feelings or content of what the speaker is saying. Using this skill demonstrates that you understand and gives the speaker the opportunity to clarify and expand. This may take the form of *"So, what you are saying is..."* or *"All right, so, my understanding of what you are saying is..."*.

You will be amazed at how effective these simple skills are in getting people to talk about their needs and feelings. You may also be surprised at how few people effectively use these skills.

Being assertive means being able to assert your own feelings and needs but also understanding the feelings and needs of others. You can choose a course of action that benefits everyone. Learning to listen is an essential skill to find out what other people really want.

Giving three-part assertion messages

When you assert yourself, you are giving a message that you want another person to respect your emotional and/or physical boundaries. The most effective assertiveness messages consist of three distinct parts:

A description of the problem. This description must be non-judgmental and should avoid any suggestion of blame. It must be sufficiently detailed and specific that the other person will clearly understand the problem. For example, "*You're a lazy slob*" is not going to evoke a positive response. "*I always end up being rushed in the morning because I have to wash up and tidy the apartment on my own*" is better because it explains precisely what is troubling you.

A description of how this makes you feel. Describe what negative emotions the problem behavior evokes in you. If it makes you anxious, stressed, frightened, or angry, say so. Don't hold back. If a behavior makes you so angry that you may lose your temper, don't be tempted to soften this statement by saying instead that it irritates you. Assertiveness is about honesty, especially in regard to your feelings.

A clarification of how the other person's behavior affects you. A description of what the other person is doing (or not doing) to cause these emotions. This explanation should be as precise as possible in order to facilitate a solution.

This description may sound complicated, but the object is to produce a message that is as concise as possible. In most cases, these three elements can be combined in a single sentence in the form: "*When you* (a description of the behavior that is making you uncomfortable), *I feel* (a description of the emotions this behavior makes you feel) *because* (a description of how this behavior directly affects you). For example, an effective three-part assertiveness message could be:

> *"When you don't get up until eight o'clock, I feel stressed and anxious because I have to do all the cleaning up before I leave for work."*

You will note that this three-part message does not impose or even suggest a solution. That is important because, if the solution is to be effective, it must take account of the feelings and needs of everyone involved. Such a solution will be most effective if it is jointly developed, not simply imposed by one side. Ideally, on being presented with the three-part assertion message, the person you are talking to will understand the problem and will suggest or contribute to a solution.

When you are rehearsing assertiveness, use this three-part message. Write down the message you want to give before you talk to the person involved. Being prepared and having thought through precisely what it is you want to say will make it much easier to be assertive.

Practical strategies for saying *"No"*

The best and most effective way to say *"No"* is to do just that. Keep it simple. Say *"No"* and stop there. That's much harder than you might think. The moment immediately after you say *"No,"* especially if you are not used to refusing anyone, will be hard for you. Saying *"No"* will create tension, and you will want to keep talking to defuse the situation. You may be tempted to offer some other form of help or assistance to make the other person feel better. This is also the time when you will be most tempted to reverse your decision. Be prepared and resist that temptation. Remember, you don't have to give excuses for saying no, and it isn't your responsibility to make the other person happy. Each time you say *"No"* and stick to it, it will get easier.

A simple and straightforward *"No"* is always the best solution to refusing something. However, if you are struggling with this, there are strategies you can use to make it easier.

> **Explain.** Saying *"No"* is an assertiveness message. You don't have to explain or justify it. However, you can use a three-part assertion message to let them clearly understand why you are saying *"No."*

> **Defer the decision.** Rather than simply saying no, you can defer making a final decision. For example, someone asks you for a favor. Instead of saying *"No,"* you could say *"I won't do that right now but get back to me later."*

> **Offer an alternative.** Suppose someone asks you for help to move from their apartment. Rather

than saying *"No,"* you could say, *"I can't be there for the whole day, but I can spare two hours."* Imagine someone invites you to a social gathering that you don't want to attend. You could say *"I can't do that this month, but I will have some free time next month."* In effect, you are offering a consolation prize, something that uses less of your time and energy or fits better with your schedule. You can benefit from this approach, and it may not be as difficult for you as a simple *"No."*

Acknowledge while refusing. Sometimes, the effect of a *"No"* can be softened by acknowledging the other person's feelings. For example, a friend asks you to go with them to a social gathering. Rather than a simple *"No"* you could say *"I know you're nervous about going on your own, but I really don't want to do that."*

Nominate someone better qualified. For example, if you are asked to give someone a lift, you could respond with *"I'm really not confident driving at night on streets I don't know. But I know that X-person is fine with that."*

Put it off. This strategy is the easiest, but also the least honest way to say *"No."* Only use this strategy if you really can't face anything more direct. This involves a response along the lines of *"Let me see how things go, and I'll get back to you."* It does not include a timescale and in truth, you have no intention of getting back to the other person. This can also be a useful strategy if someone won't take your *"No"* and keeps pestering you to change your mind.

Whichever form of *"No"* you choose to use, do not be tempted to temper your *"No"* with an apology. Most of us find *"Sorry, but no"* much easier to say than *"No."* In fact, many of us are such inveterate apologizers that we constantly say that we're sorry. That isn't appropriate when you are saying *"No."* An apology is appropriate if you have done something wrong or something to hurt or distress another person that you may feel shame about. Saying *"No"* is your right and it is not something shameful. Don't apologize when you say *"No."*

Just like other aspects of becoming assertive, saying *"No"* is a learned skill. If you are currently very passive, it's probably a skill you never practice. When you begin to use it, people who are used to taking your affirmation for granted are going to be surprised. They are probably also not going to be happy. Be ready for that. Every time you say *"No"* and stick to it, it gets easier for you and other people get used to it.

Dealing with opposition

When you give assertion messages in real life (including saying *"No"*), that often won't be the end of the story. People will almost always react defensively and try to oppose your assertion. For that reason, delivering your assertion message is only one part of a six-step process. The overall process looks like this:

1. **Prepare.** Think about what you are going to say and compose your three-part assertion message. Rehearse giving the message, and think about the behavior or situation you want to change. Is this something that can be changed? Will that change irreparably damage a relationship? Are you willing to risk that in order to get what you want?
2. **Deliver the three-part message.** Do this calmly and in a place without distraction.
3. **Stop talking**. When you have delivered the message, don't be tempted to explain or justify. Don't apologize. Just stop talking, and wait for the other person to speak.
4. **Listen.** In the real world, it is unlikely that your message will be followed by a calm acceptance by the other person and a sensible discussion of possible solutions. When people are faced by an assertion message asking them to change their behavior, most people will be surprised and perhaps unhappy. They will often immediately become defensive by seeking to justify their actions. During this phase, you must use your reflective listening skills. Let them talk.
5. **Repeat steps 2 -4** as often as required until the other person is ready to:

6. **Talk about solutions**. It is possible that listening to the other person's response may have revealed needs that they have that you may not have been aware of. Those needs may then be factored into any solution you discuss. If you can arrive at a solution that leaves you both happy, that is good. Be flexible about solutions but never lose sight of the original reason for your assertion. You are doing this because a particular situation or behavior makes you unhappy. The purpose of this assertion is to change that situation or behavior. Making the other person happy is not your main aim. Remember, you are not responsible for that person's happiness. This is about meeting your needs and any solution you agree must do that.

Some people may react to your assertion with emotions. These emotions can range from anger to unhappiness or even tears. These emotions are often a part of being initially defensive, but they may also be an attempt to manipulate you. They will pass. If the person seems so emotional that they cannot discuss the situation coherently, tell them you will discuss it again when they are feeling less emotional. At that point, repeat steps 2-6.

One of the most difficult responses is complete silence. The other person may appear angry or upset, but they say nothing. What should you do? What you should not do is go on talking. Respond to their silence by saying nothing. That's incredibly tough, and you will be tempted to end the silence but try not to. If you must say something, simply repeat your assertion message. When you can't bear the silence any longer, you may want to conclude with a statement such as *"You clearly don't want to talk about this, but I assume that you understand why I'm unhappy about* (repeat the first part of your assertion message). *We can talk about what we will do later."*

You must be prepared to persist. Simply giving an assertion message once will almost certainly not bring the change you want. You may have to repeat the assertion message anything from three to 10 times and perhaps on more than one occasion before you are able to change the situation or behavior that is affecting you. Be ready for this. Assertion messages are important. They are the only way that you change situations or behaviors to ensure that your needs and feelings are protected. Try not to become angry if you have to keep repeating the message. Becoming hostile or aggressive will not make the other person do what you want.

This process probably sounds emotionally demanding. It may be, and it will often involve some level of confrontation. Perhaps the very thought of it makes you anxious. Don't let that stop you from asserting yourself. It isn't easy but, once you learn to deliver assertiveness messages effectively, you have mastered the single most important assertiveness skill.

The four stages of becoming assertive

No one goes from being passive to assertive in a single step. Becoming assertive is a process of gradual change, of replacing your current passive behaviors with new assertive behaviors. It's going to take time, effort, and courage on your part. You can do it, and arriving at your destination will involve passing through these four stages:

Stage 1: Rehearsal and reflection

In this stage you will rehearse your new assertions skills inside your head, safely and without the risk of failure or disappointment. Think about situations where you could use those skills. Think about precisely how you could have used them in the past. Reflect on the situations and behaviors that you would most like to change. Write them down and try writing down appropriate three-part assertion messages. Don't worry. This stage is all about reflection, thinking about how and where you will use those new skills.

Stage 2: First practice

You have read this book; you understand how to become assertive, and you probably can't wait to try the new approach on the biggest problems in your life. Wait a moment! If you attempt to use your new skills in the most challenging situations involving the most intractable people, you are setting yourself up to fail. Instead, take it one small step at a time. This is a marathon, not a sprint. Initially, practice your new assertiveness skills in situations you find less stressful. Doing this may not make an instant and fundamental change to your life, but you will be practicing the skills you will use elsewhere. Only when you have tested and refined your new skills will you be ready to move on to the next stage.

Stage 3: Becoming assertive

This is it! You will be using your new skills to tackle real-life situations that may involve some level of confrontation. These are harder to deal with, but the potential rewards are greater, too. When you learn to be assertive at this level, you will understand that you are in control of your life and capable of changing what you are not happy with.

Stage 4: Prioritizing your needs

Now that you are becoming more comfortable with acting assertively, it's time to assess how you want to use these skills. What are the most significant changes you want to make in your life?

Now, let's look at a detailed 20-step plan for working through all four stages of becoming assertive.

Your 20-step assertiveness plan

This chapter provides twenty steps that will take you from passive to assertive. You can work through the steps at whatever rate you choose. You could do them on consecutive days, though that would represent quite a challenge! You could do them in a single month. If you feel that you'd rather stretch these steps out over three or six months (or even longer), that's not a problem. Make sure to work through all the steps at a pace that you are comfortable with. This book isn't about becoming assertive for one month. It is about learning skills that will sustain you through the rest of your life.

Stage 1: Rehearsal and reflection

> **Step 1.** Think about occasions in the past when a lack of assertiveness has been a problem. These are situations in which you have found yourself acting in ways that left you feeling frustrated or unfulfilled. This may have been because you did not feel able to say *"No"* or you were not able to communicate your own needs and emotions. Write them down. Be detailed and describe how these events made you feel. Find at least five examples.

> **Step 2.** For each example, write down how you reacted. Did you say nothing at the time but found yourself brooding and resentful afterwards? Did you complain to other people later but didn't speak up at the time? Don't get frustrated or blame yourself. You need to know where you are now before you can begin to

improve. This isn't about finding fault with yourself; it's about objectively looking at your reaction to this lack of assertiveness.

Step 3. For each example, write out a three-part assertion message that you could have given. Think about how giving this message instead of reacting the way that you did might have changed the outcome.

Step 4. Look at those three-part assertion messages that you have created. In particular, look at the vocabulary they use. Those messages describe how you feel. Saying this to other people is an important part of asserting your own needs. Now, think about how you could include that same vocabulary in everyday speech. Can you think of situations in which you could describe your feelings more often?

Step 5. Reflect on what you have said during the course of a given day. For example, have you apologized? Was that appropriate? Had you really done something that warranted an apology? Were there occasions when you could have mentioned how you were feeling, but you didn't? Did you experience feelings of anxiety or resentment? What caused them?

Now, you should have a much clearer picture of where you are in terms of your assertiveness or lack of it. Take as long as you need for the first stage of the action plan. It's important that you understand your current situation because that will provide motivation to change. Now, it's time to move from thinking about being assertive to taking action, though there will still be pauses for reflection in the next stage.

Stage 2: First practice

> **Step 6.** Your first assertion exercise is quite simple. You will describe to someone negative emotions you are feeling. This isn't about delivering an assertion message. It simply involves telling another person about feelings of anxiety, resentment or even anger. The person you tell may decide to talk more about these emotions or they may not. Their response is not important. This step is about learning to express negative emotions because that is something that unassertive people like people-pleasers find exceedingly difficult to do. Do this as often as you wish. The objective is to become comfortable with expressing feelings, even negative feelings. When you have done this, reflect on how expressing yourself in this way made you feel.

> **Step 7.** Fear is a major barrier to assertiveness. In this step, you will role-play refusing a request for help from someone who is insistent and demanding. If you have a trusted friend, ask them to play the role of the other person. Otherwise, play both of these roles yourself, inside your head. Imagine the situation to be as confrontational as possible. Think in detail about that the other person might say and how you could effectively respond.

Step 8. Once again, you will be role-playing, either with a friend or in your head. This time, the person making the request for help will not give up. Get used to the notion of continuing to stick to your assertion message, even repeating this time after time while remaining calm.

Step 9. Another role-play. This time it's about saying *"No"* in the fewest possible words. Find the simplest, most direct way of saying *"No"* without excuses, justification, or apologies. This is much harder than it sounds, so get comfortable with it in role-play before you begin to use this strategy in real life.

Step 10. In a safe, public setting such as a store, mall, library, or at work, make a request or ask a question of someone you don't know well. This request can be as small as asking for the time, asking for directions, or asking for help to operate a piece of equipment such as a printer. What it is will depend on your personal circumstances. The important thing to note is that if you ask with confidence, most people will be happy to oblige. If you are a very passive person, even this tiny piece of assertion will be challenging. When you have done it, reflect on how that made you feel.

Step 11. Ask a friend or someone you know well for something. Ask to borrow a stapler at work. Ask someone if they will pick up a sandwich for you. Ask someone for advice on something you're working on. Again, what you ask for will depend entirely on your personal circumstances. Make the request politely and confidently.

Step 12. This is the end of Stage 2 and you're almost ready to begin using your assertiveness skills. But first, reflect on these initial stages. What did you find most difficult? Expressing negative feelings? Asking a stranger for something? Asking a friend for something? If you found any of these especially challenging, you may want to repeat them until they become more comfortable for you before you move on to the next step.

Stage 3: Becoming assertive

Step 13. Disagree with someone. Choose a safe situation where you can offer a contrarian view. If a friend suggests going to a particular venue, disagree and suggest an alternative. If someone at work states a view on something, offer the opposite view. It doesn't really matter what the situation or how small the circumstance. You aren't being rude by doing this, just offering an alternative view. This is a great way of building your assertiveness muscles. Repeat as often as you wish.

Step 14. Repeat the above step, but use persuasion to try to get someone to agree with your view. You may be surprised at how easy this is if you are confident and calm.

Step 15. Get your own way. For example, if you are ordering food from a fixed menu, ask if you can swap one of the items for something else. Make a specific request for the food you order. Perhaps ask that your pizza is provided without olives, for example. If you are at a social gathering or meeting, ask to swap seats with someone. If they ask why, you can always say that you find the light better in that seat or the seat itself more comfortable. Once again, the precise situation is not important. What is important is that you make a request and that you use your assertive skills to get your own way.

Step 16. Repeat the step above, making more demanding requests. Be as outrageous as you want but do remember to consider other people's emotions or needs. Asking for the most comfortable chair in the room is fine, but if you have a friend or colleague who suffers from back problems, maybe they need it more. Ask for whatever you want, but not at the expense of others.

Step 17. Use a three-part assertion message as part of a six-part assertion process. This is a tough step, and it should involve a difficult conversation or even a confrontation. Perhaps it's a meeting with your boss to talk about promotion or a pay rise. Perhaps it's a discussion with a friend or partner about an element of their behavior that is causing you distress. Whether it's personal or professional, this step is about changing a situation that is causing you major distress. It's almost certainly something you haven't been looking forward to. But now, you have the skills to tackle it effectively. Rehearse your assertion message until you feel ready, and then have that conversation. Use your listening skills when the other person replies.

Step 18. Review the last step. What was the outcome? Did you get what you wanted? If not, think about why. Was there something you could have said differently or more clearly that would have changed the outcome? Did you lose confidence and back down? Most importantly, how did you feel afterwards? Even if the outcome wasn't precisely what you wanted, you should have been able to make the other person clearly understand your feelings. Did this make you feel empowered and more confident? Repeat this step as often as required.

Stage 4: Prioritizing your needs

You have now practiced all the skills you need to be assertive. You have come a long way since you started, and now it's time to think about how to use those skills to change and improve your life.

Step 19. Review your personal goals. Where do you want to go in your life? What changes do you want to make in your personal or professional life? What really matters to you? If you're passive and particularly if you were a people-pleaser, these core values can get lost amid your concern for other people's needs. It's time to get back to basics: What makes you happy? Conversely, what makes you unhappy? Write these down. These will become your goals, the situations or behaviors that you want to adopt or change. It may take some time to finalize your list, and you will probably find yourself extending it as you think of new additions.

Step 20. Plan how you can use your new assertion skills to achieve your goals. Write down your personal boundaries. Make a list of the goals you want to achieve in the next month, the next six months, and the next year. Review this list frequently and assess your progress. Update the list with new goals if you want. This list of goals will become your master plan, and assertiveness will help you to achieve it. When you are assertive, you can be whoever you want to be. You can do whatever you want to do. All you need to do now is to make the choice to become assertive.

YOUR FREE GIFT

We would like to give you a gift to thank you for purchasing this book. You can choose from any of our other published titles.

You can get immediate access to any of our books by clicking on the link below and joining our mailing list:

https://campsite.bio/mastertoday

Our other books

Mental Toughness & Discipline Mastery: *Build your Self-Confidence to Unlock your Courage and Resilience*

Build Your Self-Confidence, and Unlock Your Courage to Endure Hardship and Perform Under Any Condition!

Mental toughness will help you rise above the many people who are easily affected by their external circumstances such as challenges, obstacles, and mishaps. It allows you to perform under pressure and overcome life's challenges.

This book hands you the keys to develop true mental toughness.

Image yourself dealing with life's problems with confidence, certainty, and a lion-like courage. Picture yourself facing any issue or setback that might occur. Are you ready for that?

If yes, this mental toughness & discipline mastery book is for you!

Build your self-confidence and unlock your courage and resilience to deal with adversity... Persevere, handle the pressure, and stick to your plans. Stop draining your energy and get more out of life than you thought possible!

Toughen your mind and master your discipline, control your impulses, and endure the emotional and psychological distress that is the root cause of misfortune. Make feeling overwhelmed, exhausted, or overburdened symptoms of the past.

In **Mental Toughness & Discipline Mastery**, you will discover:

- What mental toughness is, and what it is not...
- The character traits that mentally tough people learned to rise above mediocrity.

- Why motivation and willpower are not dependable tools.
- How discipline helps you get more out of life.
- How mental toughness is the essential ingredient for success.
- The keys to strengthening your mind and unlock peak performance.
- How you can delay gratification with ease.

Become mentally tough. The book includes a step-by-step workbook and 15 powerful exercises that will help you turn what you will learn throughout this book into daily habits!

Stop giving up when life gets tough. Master your mind and discipline to become resilient. Start your training and grab your copy of this book today to face adversity with courage!

Find out more here:

https://master.today/books/mental-toughness/